101 GREAT ANSWERS
to the
TOUGHEST INTERVIEW QUESTIONS

101 GREAT ANSWERS
to the
TOUGHEST INTERVIEW QUESTIONS

Ron Fry

THOMSON
DELMAR LEARNING

Australia Brazil Canada Mexico Singapore Spain United Kingdom United States

THOMSON
DELMAR LEARNING

101 Great Answers to the Toughest Interview Questions
Ron Fry

Vice President, Career Education SBU: Dawn Gerrain	Director of Production: Wendy A. Troeger	Director of Marketing: Wendy E. Mapstone
Director of Learning Solutions: Sherry Dickinson	Production Manager: J.P. Henkel	Channel Manager: Gerard McAvey
Managing Editor: Robert L. Serenka, Jr.	Production Editor: Rebecca Goldthwaite	Marketing Specialist: Erica Conley

Acquisitions Editor:
Martine Edwards

Developmental Editor:
Jennifer Anderson

Editorial Assistant:
Falon Ferraro

For permission to use material from this text or product, submit a request online at http://www.thomsonrights.com

Any additional questions about permissions can be submitted by email to thomsonrights@thomson.com

Library of Congress Cataloging-in-Publication Data
Fry, Ronald W.
    101 great answers to the toughest interview questions / Ron Fry.—5th ed.
        p. cm.
    ISBN-13: 978-1-4180-4000-0
    ISBN-10: 1-4180-4000-2
    1. Employment interviewing.
    I. Title: One-hundred-and-one great answers to the toughest interview questions. II. Title.
    HF5549.5.I6F75 2006
    650.14'4—dc22
                                        2006008005

NOTICE TO THE READER

Publisher does not warrant or guarantee any of the products described herein or perform any independent analysis in connection with any of the product information contained herein. Publisher does not assume, and expressly disclaims, any obligation to obtain and include information other than that provided to it by the manufacturer.

The reader is expressly warned to consider and adopt all safety precautions that might be indicated by the activities herein and to avoid all potential hazards. By following the instructions contained herein, the reader willingly assumes all risks in connection with such instructions.

The Publisher makes no representation or warranties of any kind, including but not limited to, the warranties of fitness for particular purpose or merchantability, nor are any such representations implied with respect to the material set forth herein, and the publisher takes no responsibility with respect to such material. The publisher shall not be liable for any special, consequential, or exemplary damages resulting, in whole or part, from the readers' use of, or reliance upon, this material.

The authors and Thomson Delmar Learning affirm that the Web site URLs referenced herein were accurate at the time of printing. However, due to the fluid nature of the Internet, we cannot guarantee their accuracy for the life of the edition.

CONTENTS

INTRODUCTION

One, Two, Three . . . Green Light!

I n the nearly fifteen years since I wrote the first edition of **101 Great Answers to the Toughest Interview Questions,** its relevance to an ever-changing job market has continued to grow. That market has certainly changed—from a seller's (employee-friendly) market to a buyer's (employer-friendly) market and back again. But the power this book has given interviewees, whatever their ages, skills, or qualifications, has expanded every year.

I certainly couldn't boast of my own interviewing skills before I wrote this book. On the contrary, I had often *not* gotten jobs for which I was eminently qualified. So I spent quite a lot of time learning all the mistakes you could possibly make, having made each one of them—twice.

Now, as a veteran of the other side of the desk as well (I've hired hundreds and interviewed thousands), I can tell you that interviewing is more serious business than ever before.

Employers are looking for self-managing employees—people who are versatile, confident, ready and able to work with a team, and not afraid to roll up their sleeves, work long hours, and get the job done. "That's me," you chortle. Congratulations. But you won't get the chance to prove yourself on the job without making it through the interview process.

Interviewing was never easy, and right now it is harder than ever. Companies are taking far longer to make hiring decisions, and then only after putting prospective employees through more and longer interviews. One search firm reports that many candidates have had to interview a half dozen times or more for a single position.

But of all the tools in your professional arsenal, your ability to shine in that brief moment in time—your first interview—can make or break your chances for a second go-around and, ultimately, dictate whether you're ever given a shot at the job.

HOW DO YOU GET TO CARNEGIE HALL?

Like playing the piano, interviewing takes practice, and practice makes perfect. The hours of personal interviewing experience, both the tragedies and the triumphs, as well as my years as an interviewer, are the basis for this book. I hope to spare you many of the indignities I suffered along the way, by helping you prepare for the interview of your worst nightmares—at a comfortable remove from the interviewer's glare.

Will you have to answer every question I've included? Certainly not; at least not in a single interview. But chances are the questions tomorrow's interviewer _doesn't_ ask will be on the tip of the _next_ interviewer's tongue. Why? It's a mystery.

HOW TO PAINT A PICTURE

Most interviewers are not trying to torture you for sport. Their motive is to quickly learn enough about you to make an informed decision—should you stay or should you go? By the same token, if you know what they're looking for, you can craft your answers accordingly (and reduce your own fear and anxiety at the same time).

I hope you'll take it a step further and use these questions as the basis for some thoughtful self-exploration. You'll need to be prepared to think for yourself—on your feet, not by the seat of your pants.

While competitive, certainly, the interview process is not a competition. Rather than thinking of yourself as an athlete trying to "out answer" the other candidates, consider an interview your chance to be an artist, to paint a portrait of the person you are, the kind of candidate any company would like, respect, . . . and want to hire.

Chapters 1 and 2 offer a detailed discussion of the work you need to do and the things you need to think about long before you strut into your first interview. Interviewing may not be 99 percent preparation, but it's certainly 50 percent.

In Chapters 3 through 10, we'll get into the meat of the book—the questions for which you must prepare and the answers most interviewers are hoping to hear. (I have not counted every question in this book, from the main ones to the variations, but there are now far more than the 101 still advertised on the cover.) Each question is generally followed by a series of three subheadings:

 ## WHAT DO THEY WANT TO HEAR?

(What information is the interviewer seeking?)

 ### GREEN LIGHT
(What's a good answer?)

 ### RED LIGHT
(What's a poor answer?)

I've listed follow-up questions you should expect or variations an interviewer may substitute after many of the questions.

The questions in this book are grouped by type; they are not in some suggested order. Many of the questions in Chapters 8 or 10, for example, may well be some of the first questions asked in every interview! So read the entire book and prepare for *all* of the questions in *any* order.

Despite the emphasis on "great answers," I do *not* recommend rote memorization. Trotting out a staged, textbook answer to a question is not the point of the interview process . . . or of this book. It is actually more important to concentrate on the "What do they want to hear?" section after each question, to have an understanding of *why* the interviewer is asking a particular question and what you need to do to frame a winning answer.

The "red lights" after many of the questions indicate answers that will make the average interviewer cringe and the busy interviewer simply suggest you try another firm.

After almost every question in the book, however, I could have included the same list of general red lights, those factors that should be avoided in any interview or in the answer to any question. So as not to unnecessarily clutter up the book, let's discuss these all-encompassing negatives right here.

OH, DID I FORGET TO CALL?

For many interviewers, your showing up late is immediate cause for canceling the interview. It doesn't matter that traffic backed up, your cat threw up a hairball, or you just got lost in the elevator.

Being on time is not racing down the final corridor with moments to spare. Some interviewers agree with New York Giants football coach Tom Coughlin—being late is not being fifteen minutes *early*.

NICE HAIR . . . AND LOVE THE LIPSTICK

Poor grooming is a basic turn-off. Wearing so much perfume or cologne that a gasping interviewer lunges for the window is a bad way to start. So is wearing more makeup than a runway model, clanking along with a pocketful of change or an armload of bangles and bells, or doing your best Richard Nixon five o'clock shadow impression.

You may have pertinent skills and experience . . . heck, you may be *perfect* for the job . . . but never get the chance to tout your credentials if your grooming makes a poor first impression.

UH, DOES THAT TIE GLOW IN THE DARK?

Do I really have to tell you, ladies, that a dark suit, pearls, and pumps is appropriate dress for every interview? Given the tube tops, sneakers, short skirts, and patterned stockings I've seen waltz through my door (and all on one candidate!), maybe I do.

For men: white or light blue shirt, conservative suit, silk tie, shined dress shoes.

For *no one:* ties that glow in the dark, T-shirts advertising anything (but especially not X-rated!), or any clothes deemed "relaxed and comfortable" (unless you are relaxed and comfortable in a double-breasted suit).

ARE YOU A TOBACCO FARMER?

In case you haven't gotten the message (where have you been?), smoking is no longer acceptable behavior . . . anywhere, any time. And don't kid yourselves; just because you don't light up during an interview doesn't mean that everyone in the room doesn't know you smoke, You reek, bro!

If you smoke, stop. Not just the morning of the interview. Stop. There are many companies that won't want to hire you because of the additional health risks you bring to the table. Or just because they don't want to deal with the downtime as you head off once an hour for that attractive corner beside the front door.

Of course, if you decide to smoke during the interview itself (and some people have in my office) you can go down to that front door right away to finish up.

Do not smoke even if the interviewer lights up and encourages you to do likewise.

YOU BROUGHT YOUR CAT. HOW NICE.

There should be a new reality series featuring the bizarre behavior of some interviewees, as they chew, burp, scratch, swear, cry, laugh, and scream their way into our hearts. Interviewees have shown up drunk or stoned, brought their mothers with them, fallen asleep, and even gone to the bathroom and never returned.

Keeping your cell phone on during the interview qualifies as inappropriate behavior. Actually receiving or making a call ranks as bizarre.

Remember what the interviewer is thinking: If this is your *best* behavior, what (*gasp!*) do I have to look forward to?

THEY DON'T NEED A LIE DETECTOR

If you lie about anything, especially where and when you worked, what you did, where and when (or even if) you attended college, you will be caught. No matter how lowly the job, there are significant expenses involved with hiring someone to perform it. So companies will take the time to check out references. And the higher up the food chain, the more intensive their scrutiny.

Even if the lie is inconsequential, the very fact that you lied will, in virtually all instances, be immediate grounds for dismissal. Lacking a particular skill or experience may not automatically exclude you from getting the job. Lying about it will.

I DON'T NEED YOU TO BE *THAT* HONEST

While honesty may be the best (and only) policy, it is not necessary to share anything and everything with your interviewer. He is not your priest, and you are not in a confessional. Anything you do in the privacy of your own home is not something you need to share.

And do be smart enough when asked what interests you about the job not to answer, "Heck, I just need a job with benefits. I owe way too much on my Visa."

"LAST JOB? HATED IT!"

You should attempt to make every minute of your interview a positive experience. In fact, introducing negativity of any kind is virtually guaranteed to dim your chances. (Which is why the *interviewer* may introduce negativity, just to see how you handle it.) So complaining about your last job, boss, duties, or even the elevator ride upstairs, should be avoided at all costs.

UH, LOOK OVER HERE PLEASE

To many interviewers, your failure to look them in the eye indicates you have something to hide. So does being overly fidgety or nervous. Greet the interviewer with a firm handshake, face him or her, sit straight up, and, of course, look 'em in the eye. *Breaking* eye contact occasionally is also a good idea. Staring at someone without pause for more than a few seconds will make them nervous.

Likewise, interviewers are looking for people who are enthusiastic about what they do, so sighing, looking out the window, or checking your watch during a question is not creating the right impression. If you don't seem interested in the job, why should they be interested in hiring you?

Don't underestimate the effect of your body language on the interviewer. While many people don't mean what they say or say what they mean, their nonverbal actions reveal *exactly* what they're feeling. According to studies, *more than half* of what we are trying to communicate is being received nonverbally.

You need to understand not only what your own body language is communicating to the interviewer, but what you can learn from his or hers. If he crosses his arms or leans back in the chair, you've lost him. But if she's leaning forward, nodding while you speak, and gesturing when she does, you're keeping her interested. Don't overanalyze the situation. An interviewer vigorously rubbing her eyes may just be telling you . . . she didn't get enough sleep last night.

YOU CAN BE A BIT *TOO* CONFIDENT

A candidate once said to me, barely five minutes into our interview, "I've got three other offers right now. What can you do for me?"

I showed him the door.

Yes, you need to be confident, enthusiastic, and cheerful (and brave and clean and reverent), but you can be, as this example clearly illustrates, too much of a good thing.

"UH, WHY DO YOU WANT TO KNOW?"

The interviewer asks what she thinks is a simple question, and you act as if she has accused you of a crime. You start to sweat, hem and haw, and try to change the subject.

What are you hiding? That's what the interviewer will be thinking. And if you aren't actually hiding anything, why are you acting so defensively?

"WHAT DOES THIS COMPANY DO?"

A key part of the interview process is preparation—researching the company, industry, and position; preparing pertinent questions; being ready to sprinkle your knowledge into the conversation. So failing to do any of this will not impress most interviewers. I *have* had candidates ask me what exactly my company did.

Not hire *them*.

"SURE, BOB, YOU CAN HAVE THE LOBSTER."

Just don't expect to also get the job.

Interviewing over lunch is a situation fraught with potential dangers. Slurping spaghetti or wiping barbecue sauce off your tie is simply not attractive, even if you are. Ordering the most (or least) expensive item on the menu sends an unwelcome message. And what happens when the French dish you didn't understand but ordered anyway turns out to be sautéed brains?

If you can't avoid a lunch interview (and I would certainly try), use your common sense. Order something light and reasonably priced; you're not *really* there for the food, are you? Remember what Mom told you—keep your elbows off the table, don't talk with your mouth full, and put your napkin on your lap. Don't drink alcohol (even wine), don't smoke (even if your host does), don't complain about the food (even if it was lousy), and don't forget that this is still an interview!

"AND THEN I WORKED FOR . . . OOPS!"

Throughout this book, I have attempted to give you the ability to formulate answers that respond to what the interviewer *really* wants to know. The more responsive your answer is to the interviewer's stated (or unstated) needs, the better. Since the best answers are customized to fit the company's needs and your qualifications, it's often difficult, if not impossible, to say that a particular answer is right or wrong. But there are answers that *are* clearly wrong:

- Any answer, no matter how articulate and specific, that fails to actually answer the question asked.

- Any answer that reveals you are clearly unqualified for the job.

- Any answer that provides information that doesn't jibe with your resume and/or cover letter. (Don't laugh. I, for one, have proudly given details about a job I left off my resume. The interviewer didn't laugh either.)

- Any answer that reveals an inability to take responsibility for failures/weaknesses/bad decisions/bad results, or one that tries to take full credit for a project to which others clearly contributed.

Although many interviewers will not consider inappropriate dress, poor grooming, or a bit too much candor an automatic reason for dismissal, an accumulation of two or more such actions may force even the most empathetic to question your suitability. (Some items, of course, such as dishonesty, may well lead to an immediate and heartfelt, "Thank you . . . see you.")

PLEASE USE A NO. 2 PENCIL

More and more employers are subjecting candidates to personality tests before they even get a chance to meet a live interviewer. According to author and speaker Jane Boucher, more than 65 percent of Fortune 500 companies use some kind of assessment test for both hourly workers and managers, up from only five percent less than a decade ago.

I know from experience that you cannot "beat" these tests. If you try to choose the answers you believe are "obviously" the ones showing your leadership skills, you will not succeed. Since you can't really prepare for any such tests, relax and try to answer the questions honestly. Most of these tests are merely trying to identify the jobs for which your personality type is best suited. And at most companies, they are only one component of the interview process.

PAUSE FOR SELF-CONGRATULATIONS

Despite my sterling reputation with employment offices, the first edition of this book became a bestseller. In fact, it continues to sell, year after year. I don't pretend to know why it has done as well as it has, but I will hazard a guess: It's simple, straightforward, practical, and written in a welcoming and humorous style. (Okay, I suppose that counts as four and a half guesses.) And it has clearly helped literally hundreds of thousands of candidates prepare for every type of interview and every style of interviewer. I'm pleased and proud that this new edition will help many more of you!

Rather than spend a lot more time telling you what you're going to learn, let's just get you started. Good luck.

—Ron Fry

P.S. I almost forgot to mention the usage of gender throughout this book. Instead of being gender-biased, I've chosen to split the difference and mix up the usage of "he/him" and "she/her" wherever it doesn't get too cumbersome.

CHAPTER

The Product Is You

The object of this chapter is to prepare you to comfortably
answer one—and *only* one—question: "Who are you?"
The success or failure of many interviews will hinge on your
ability to answer this seemingly simple question. The interviewing process is a kind of sale. In this case, *you* are the product—
and the salesperson. If you show up unprepared to talk about
your unique features and benefits, you're not likely to motivate
an interviewer to "buy."

The sad fact is that many job candidates *are* unprepared to
talk about themselves. You may have mailed a gorgeous resume
and cover letter. You may be wearing the perfect clothes on the
day of the interview. But if you can't convince the interviewer,
face to face, that *you* are the right person for the job, you aren't
likely to make the sale.

Too many candidates hesitate after the first open-ended
question, then stumble and stutter their way through a disjointed litany of resume sound bites. Other interviewees recite
canned replies that only highlight their memory skills.

I am assuming that, like most people, you are a complex product made up of a unique blend of abilities, skills, and personal qualities, one shaped by your own personal and professional history. Believe me, the time you spend outlining the details of your own life will pay off in interviews and, ultimately, job offers. This chapter will guide you through the process.

WHAT YOU SHOULD KNOW ABOUT YOU

Your first step is to imitate the FBI and build a complete dossier on yourself. The Data Input Sheets at the end of this chapter will help you organize important information about yourself. With this information in place, it will be easier to develop a concise and convincing answer to almost any interview question—an answer that will set you apart from the competition. (I've only included one copy of each form. Feel free to reproduce as many as you need.)

EMPLOYMENT DATA INPUT SHEET

Prepare a separate sheet for every full-time and part-time job you have ever held, no matter how short the tenure. Yes, even summer jobs are important here. They demonstrate resourcefulness, responsibility, and initiative, that you were already developing a sense of independence while you were still living at home. Whether you choose to include some, all, or none of these short-term jobs on your resume or to discuss them during your interview are decisions you will make later. For now, write down everything about *every* job. For each employer, include:

- Name, address, telephone number, and E-mail address.

- The names of all of your supervisors and, whenever possible, where they can be reached.

- Letters of recommendation (especially if they *can't* be reached).

- The exact dates (month and year) you were employed.

For each job, include:

- Specific duties and responsibilities.

- Supervisory experience, noting the number of people you managed.

- Specific skills required for the job.

- Key accomplishments.

- Dates you received promotions.

- Any awards, honors, or special recognition you received.

For each part-time job, also include:

- The number of hours you worked per week.

You don't need to write a *book* on each job, but do concentrate on providing *specific data* (volume of work handled, problems solved, dollars saved) to paint a *detailed* picture of your abilities and accomplishments. Believe me, these hard facts will add a powerful punch to your interview presentation.

Duties: Write one or two sentences giving an overview of the tasks you handled in each of the jobs you held. Use numbers as often as possible to demonstrate the scope of your responsibilities. An experienced salesperson might write:

- Responsible for managing 120 active accounts in sales territory that contributed $3 million in annual revenues.

- Reviewed activity of three telephone salespeople.

Skills: Name the specific skills required to perform your duties, highlighting those that you developed on the job. The same salesperson might write:

- Trained other sales staff in new product lines.

- Handled telephone support for customer base of 100.

Key accomplishments: This is the place to "brag," but be sure to back up each accomplishment with specifics, including results. For example:

- Developed new call-reporting system that increased volume in territory 20 percent within 18 months.

- Oversaw computerization of department that helped realize cost savings of 15 percent.

VOLUNTEER WORK DATA INPUT SHEET

Having hired hundreds of people during my career, I can assure you that your after-hours activities will be considered and weighed by many interviewers. Workaholics rarely make the best employees.

So take some time to make a detailed record of your volunteer pursuits, similar to the one you've just completed for each job you've held. For each volunteer organization, include:

- Name, address, telephone number, and E-mail address.

- Name of your supervisor or the director of the organization.

- Letter(s) of recommendation.

- Exact dates (month and year) of your involvement with the organization.

For each volunteer experience, include:

- Approximate number of hours devoted to the activity each month.

- Specific duties and responsibilities.

- Skills required.

- Major accomplishments.

- Awards, honors, or special recognition you received.

EDUCATIONAL DATA INPUT SHEETS

If you're a recent college graduate or are still in college, you don't need to rehash your high school experiences. If you have a graduate degree or are a graduate student, however, you should list both graduate and undergraduate course work. If you're still in school and graduation is more than a year away, indicate the number of credits you've earned through the most recent semester completed.

ACTIVITIES DATA INPUT SHEET

I'm always interested in—and impressed by—candidates who talk about books they've read and activities they've enjoyed. So make a list of all the sports, clubs, and other activities in which you've participated, inside or outside of school. For each activity, club, or group, include:

- Name and purpose.

- Offices you held; special committees you formed, chaired, or participated in; or specific positions you played.

- Duties and responsibilities of each role.

- Key accomplishments.

- Awards or honors you received.

AWARDS AND HONORS DATA INPUT SHEET

List all the awards and honors you've received from school(s), community groups, church groups, clubs, and so on. You may include awards from prestigious high schools (prep schools or professional schools) even if you're in graduate school or long out of college.

MILITARY SERVICE DATA INPUT SHEET

Many employers are impressed by the maturity of candidates who have served in the armed forces; they consider military service excellent management training for many civilian jobs. So if you've served in the armed forces, even for a short time, make sure you can discuss your experiences and how they tie into your professional aspirations. Be sure to include:

- Final rank awarded.

- Duties and responsibilities.

- Citations and awards.

- Details on specific training and/or any special schooling.

- Special skills developed.

- Key accomplishments.

LANGUAGE DATA INPUT SHEET

Even if you're not applying for a job in the international arena, your ability to read, write, and/or speak additional languages can make you invaluable to employers in an increasing number of research and educational institutions and multinational companies. One year of college Russian won't cut it. But if you spent a year studying in Moscow—and can carry on a conversation like a native—by all means write it down.

PUTTING IT IN *YOUR* PERSPECTIVE

Once you've finished completing these forms, you'll have listed a lot of facts about what you've done and where and with whom you've done it. But any interviewer worth his or her pepper will be looking for more. So once you've finished with the fact-finding, practice putting it all into perspective—your unique, personal perspective, that is. Write down your answers to the following questions, those which you should expect an interviewer will ask:

- Which achievements did you enjoy most? Which are you proudest of? Be ready to tell the interviewer how these accomplishments relate to the position at hand.

- What mistakes have you made? Why did they occur? How have you learned from them? What have you done to keep similar things from occurring again?

- How well do you interact with authority figures—bosses, teachers, parents? Be ready to furnish specific examples.

- What are your favorite games and sports? Are you overly competitive? Do you give up too easily? Are you a good loser—or a bad winner? Do you rise to a challenge or back away from it?

- What kinds of people are your friends? Do you associate only with people who are very similar to you? Do you enjoy differences in others—or merely tolerate them? What are some things that have caused you to end friendships? What does this say about you?

- If you were to ask a group of friends and acquaintances to describe you, what adjectives would they use? List all of them—the good and the bad. Why would people describe you this way? Are there specific behaviors, skills, achievements, or failures that seem to identify you in the eyes of others? What are they?

WHAT'S THE POINT?

The better you know yourself, the better you can sell yourself to a prospective employer when you're on the spot in an interview. From your Data Input Sheets, you can compile a list of your best features under the following headings:

- My strongest skills.

- My greatest areas of knowledge.

- My greatest personality strengths.

- The things I do best.

- My key accomplishments.

Then you can transform your best features into benefits for your prospective company:

- What in my personal inventory will convince this employer that I deserve the position?

- What are the strengths, achievements, skills, and areas of knowledge that make me *most* qualified for this position? What in my background should separate me from the herd of other applicants?

By answering some tough questions about the mistakes you have made, and about the less-than-positive feedback you've gotten, you can also locate areas that may need improvement. Do you need to develop new skills or improve your relations with those in authority? If you have been thorough and brutally honest (and it may feel brutal!), you may find out things about yourself that you never knew.

The more time and effort you invest in answering questions like these—while you have a cool head—the less you'll sweat once you're in the interviewer's hot seat. It's up to you.

But before we forge ahead to the first of the questions you're likely to field, let's take a closer look at the interview process itself.

Employment Data Input Sheet

Employer Name: _____

Address: _____

_____

_____

Phone: _____

E-mail: _____

Dates of Employment: _____ to _____

Hours Per Week: _____ Salary/Pay: _____

Supervisor's Name & Title: _____

Duties: _____

_____

_____

_____

_____

Skills Utilized: _____

_____

_____

_____

_____

Accomplishments/Honors/Awards: _____

_____

_____

Other Important Information: _____

_____

_____

Volunteer Work Data Input Sheet

Organization Name: _____

Address: _____

_____

_____

Phone: _____

Hours Per Week: _____

Dates of Activity: _____ to _____

Supervisor's Name & Title: _____

E-mail: _____

Duties: _____

_____

_____

_____

Skills Utilized: _____

_____

_____

_____

Accomplishments/Honors/Awards: _____

_____

_____

Other Important Information: _____

_____

_____

High School Data Input Sheet

School Name: _____

Address: _____

_____

_____

Phone: _____

Years Attended: _____ to _____

Major Studies: _____

_____

_____

GPA/Class Rank: _____

Honors: _____

_____

_____

_____

Important Courses: _____

_____

_____

_____

Other School Data Input Sheet

School Name: _____

Address: _____

_____

_____

Phone: _____

Years Attended: _____ to _____

Major Studies: _____

_____

_____

GPA/Class Rank: _____

Honors: _____

_____

_____

_____

Important Courses: _____

_____

_____

_____

College Data Input Sheet

School Name: _____

Address: _____

_____

_____

Phone: _____

Years Attended: _____ to _____

Degrees Earned: _____

Major/Minor: _____

_____

GPA/Class Rank: _____

Honors: _____

_____

_____

_____

Important Courses: _____

_____

_____

_____

Graduate School Data Input Sheet

School Name: _____

Address: _____

_____

_____

Phone: _____

Years Attended: _____ to _____

Degrees Earned: _____

Major/Minor: _____

_____

GPA/Class Rank: _____

Honors: _____

_____

_____

_____

Important Courses: _____

_____

_____

_____

Activities Data Input Sheet

Club/Activity: _____

Office(s) Held: _____

Description of Participation: _____

_____

_____

Duties/Responsibilities: _____

_____

_____

Club/Activity: _____

Office(s) Held: _____

Description of Participation: _____

_____

_____

Duties/Responsibilities: _____

_____

Club/Activity: _____

Office(s) Held: _____

Description of Participation: _____

_____

_____

Duties/Responsibilities: _____

_____

_____

Awards & Honors Data Input Sheet

Name of Award, Citation, etc.: _____

From Whom Received: _____

Date: _____

Significance: _____

_____

Other Pertinent Information: _____

_____

_____

Name of Award, Citation, etc.: _____

From Whom Received: _____

Date: _____

Significance: _____

_____

Other Pertinent Information: _____

_____

_____

Name of Award, Citation, etc.: _____

From Whom Received: _____

Date: _____

Significance: _____

_____

Other Pertinent Information: _____

_____

_____

Military Service Data Input Sheet

Branch: _____

Rank (at Discharge): _____

Dates of Service: _____ to _____

Duties & Responsibilities: _____

_____

_____

_____

Special Training and/or School Attended: _____

_____

_____

_____

Citations, Awards, etc.: _____

_____

_____

Specific Accomplishments: _____

_____

_____

_____

_____

Language Data Input Sheet

Language: _____

❏ Read   ❏ Write   ❏ Converse

Background (number of years studied, travel, etc.): _____

_____

_____

_____

Language: _____

❏ Read   ❏ Write   ❏ Converse

Background (number of years studied, travel, etc.): _____

_____

_____

_____

Language: _____

❏ Read   ❏ Write   ❏ Converse

Background (number of years studied, travel, etc.): _____

_____

_____

_____

It's Still a Jungle Out There

The days of filling out a standard application and chatting your way through one or two interviews are gone. These days, interviewers and hiring managers are reluctant to leave anything to chance.

As I mentioned previously, you'll probably have to go through more interviews than your predecessors for the same job, no matter what your level of expertise. Knowledge and experience still give you an inside edge. But these days, you'll need stamina, too. Your honesty, your intelligence, your mental health—even the toxicity of your blood—may be measured before you can be considered fully assessed.

You may also have to tiptoe through a minefield of different types of interview situations.

Don't go out and subscribe to a Human Resources journal. Just do all you can to remain confident and flexible—and ready with your answers. No matter what kind of interview you find yourself facing, this approach should carry you through with flying colors.

Let's take a brief, no-consequences tour of the interview circuit.

 ## WHAT (WHO) ARE YOU UP AGAINST?

There are three predominant interviewing types: the Telephone Screener, the Human Screen, and the Manager. Let's look at each of these types and how you should approach them.

THE TELEPHONE SCREENER

Telephone screening is an effective tactic used by many interviewers of all three types. However, people in this first group rely on the strategy as a primary means of exploring employment possibilities. For many of these interviewers, the in-person interview is little more than an opportunity to confirm what they feel they've already learned on the phone.

Interviewers who typically fall into this category are entrepreneurs, CEOs, high-level executives, and others short on time and long on vision. Their guiding philosophy could be summed up as, "I have a personnel problem to solve, and I don't plan to waste my valuable time talking in person to anybody but the very best."

The telephone screener is often the dominant interviewer at small- to mid-sized companies (where no formal Human Resources or Personnel department exists or where such a department has only recently been created). *The primary objective of the telephone screener is to identify reasons to **remove** you from active consideration before scheduling an in-person meeting.*

Among the common reasons for abrupt removal from the telephone screener's short list: evidence that there's a disparity between your resume and actual experience; poor verbal communication skills; or lack of required technical skills.

If you are expecting a call (or calls) from telephone screeners, make sure family members know how to answer the phone. Hint: A sullen "Huh?" from your teenage son is not the best way. And by all means avoid cutesy answering machine tapes. ("Hi!" [giggle, giggle] "We're upstairs getting our groove on!" [giggle, snort] "So leave a message, dude.")

Conversations with the oh-so-busy telephone screener are often quite abrupt. These people tend to have a lot on their plates.

But what could be better than answering questions from the comfort of your home, right?

Wrong! For starters, you've lost at least two valuable tools you have to work with during in-office interviews: eye contact and body language. You're left with your skills, your resume, and your ability to communicate verbally.

Don't be discouraged. Always project a positive image through your voice and your answers. Don't overdo it, but don't let the telephone be your undoing either. If your confidence is flagging, try smiling while you listen and speak. Sure, it might look silly, but it works. I also like to stand, even walk around, during a telephone interview. It seems to calm me down and give me more energy at the same time.

You have a right to be prepared for any interview. Chances are, the interviewer will call you to set a time for the telephone interview. However, if she wants to plow right into it as soon as you answer the phone, there's nothing wrong with asking if she could call back at a mutually agreeable time. You need to prepare your surroundings for a successful interview.

Next to the phone, you'll want to have a copy of your resume (which you've quickly reviewed), the cover letter you sent to that company, a list of questions *you've* prepared for *them,* a notepad, your research materials on that company, and a glass of water. You will also want to have already answered nature's call (since you surely don't want to excuse yourself in the middle of the interview) and placed a "Do Not Disturb" sign on your door so family members or roommates don't interrupt. Needless to say, you never want to put the interviewer on hold for any reason.

THE HUMAN SCREEN

Many Human Resource and Personnel professionals fall into this category. For these people, interviewing is not simply just a once-a-quarter or once-a-month event, but a key part of their daily job description. They meet and interview many people, and they are more likely than either of the other two categories to consider an exceptional applicant for more than one possible opening within the organization.

A primary objective of the human screen is to develop a strong group of candidates for managers (see category three) to interview in person. To do this, of course, they must fend off many applicants and callers, a daunting task because the human screen or the department in which he or she works is often the only contact provided in employment advertisements.

Among the most common reasons for removal from the human screen's "hot" list are: lack of formal or informal qualifications as outlined in the organization's job description; sudden changes in hiring priorities and personnel requirements; poor performance during the in-person interview itself; and inaction due to the human screen's uncertainty about your current status or contact information. That last reason is more common than you might imagine. human screens are constantly swamped with phone calls, resumes, and unannounced visits from hopeful applicants. Despite their best efforts, they sometimes lose track of qualified people.

Human screens excel at separating the wheat from the chaff. Because they are exposed to a wide variety of candidates on a regular basis, they usually boast more face-to-face interviewing experience than members of the other two groups. Human screens may be more likely to spot inconsistencies or outright lies on resumes, simply because they've seen so many over the years that they know when a candidate's credentials for a given position don't quite pass the "smell test."

And while interviews with telephone screeners or managers may be rushed to accommodate hectic schedules, human screens are generally in a position to spend comparatively long amounts of time with particularly qualified candidates.

However, these interviewers often do not have direct knowledge of the day-to-day requirements of the job to be filled. They have formal summaries, of course, but they usually don't possess the same first-hand familiarity with the skills, temperament, and outlook necessary for success on the job. Typically one step away from the action, they're reliant on job postings and experience summaries (often composed by managers).

If those formal outlines are imperfectly written, and if human screens receive no direct input from supervisors on the kinds of people they're looking for, you may be passed through the process even though you're not particularly qualified (or eliminated even though you are).

Not surprisingly, human screens often react with a puzzled look when asked by others to offer their gut reaction on the merits of a particular candidate. Because they're generally operating at a remove from the work itself, they often prefer quantifying their assessments of candidates in hard numbers: either the candidate *does* have three years doing x, y, or z, or she *doesn't*. Either she *has* been trained in computer design, or she *hasn't*. Of course, this analysis may overlook important interpersonal issues.

THE MANAGER

This category describes supervisors who choose to (or are required to) fit in-person interviews into their busy working days. Typically, they are interviewing applicants they themselves will oversee. Frequently, the interviews are the result of referrals from a human screen or from colleagues and personal contacts.

The primary objective of the manager is to evaluate the skills and personal chemistry of the applicant on a first-hand basis. These interviewers want to get to know everything they can about the people with whom they'll be working closely. (The telephone screener, in contrast, may well be an entrepreneur who delegates heavily and interacts only intermittently with new hires.)

Common reasons for being dropped from the manager's "hot" list include: lack of personal chemistry or rapport with the manager; poor performance during the interview itself; and the manager's assessment that you, although qualified and personable, would not fit in well with the team.

Often, these are the people with direct supervisory experience in the area in which the opening has arisen. A manager who has worked with a number of previous employees who held the same position brings a unique perspective to the proceedings.

Of the three categories, this is the group most likely to (mis)use the interview as an opportunity simply to get to know more about you—rather than to require specific answers to questions about your background, experience, outlook on work, and interpersonal skills.

Such interviewers often have an excellent intuitive sense of who will (and won't) be likely to perform the job well and achieve a good fit with the rest of the work group. On the other hand, it sometimes comes as a surprise to applicants that excellent supervisors can be less than stellar interviewers. But many managers lack any formal training in the art of interviewing.

Experienced interviewers are trained to stay in charge of the interview, not let it meander down some dead-end, nonproductive track. There is a predictability to the way they conduct interviews, even when they wield different techniques.

On the other hand, the hiring manager is sure to lack some or all of the screening interviewer's knowledge, experience, and skill—making him or her an unpredictable animal.

The vast majority of corporate managers don't know what it takes to hire the right candidate. Few of them have had formal training in conducting interviews of any kind. To make things worse, most managers feel slightly less comfortable conducting the interview than the nervous candidate sitting across the desk from them!

For example, a manager might decide you are not the right person for the job, without ever realizing that the questions he or she asked were so ambiguous, or so off the mark, that even the perfect candidate could not have returned the "right" answer. No one monitors the performance of the interviewer. And the candidate cannot be a mind reader. So more often than is necessary, otherwise perfectly qualified candidates walk out the door for good simply because the *manager* failed at the interview!

FOILING THE INEPT INTERVIEWER

But that doesn't have to happen to you. You can—and should—be prepared to put your best foot forward, no matter what the manager who is interviewing you does or says. That begins with having the answers to 101 questions at the ready. But it doesn't stop there; the interviewer may not ask any of these questions.

What do you do then? In the chapters that follow, you'll see how you can convince even the densest of managers that you are the best person for the job.

Simply put, you will be a step ahead of the game if you realize at the outset that managers who are interviewing to hire are seeking more than just facts about your skills and background. They are waiting for something more elusive to hit them, something they themselves may not be able to articulate. They want to feel that somehow you "fit" the organization or department.

Talk about a tough hurdle! But knowing what you're up against is half the battle. Rather than sit back passively and hope for the best, you can help the unskilled interviewer focus on how your unique skills can directly benefit—"fit"—the department or organization by using a number of specific examples.

One word of caution: Don't come on so strong that you seem to be waging a campaign. You will come off as overzealous and self-serving. You'll lose. Just keep quietly and confidently underlining the facts (your expertise) and enthusiastically showing (discovering together with the interviewer) how well these "puzzle pieces" seem to fit the job at hand.

What other unusual problems could you face during an interview?

THE "IT'S ALL ABOUT ME" INTERVIEWER

Bob thinks he's a pretty good interviewer. He has a list of 15 questions he asks every candidate—same questions, same order, every time. He takes notes on their answers, and asks an occasional follow-up question. He gives them a chance to ask questions. He's friendly, humorous, and excited about working at Netcorp.com (as he tells every candidate . . . in detail . . . for *hours*). Then he wonders why only a small fraction of his hires pan out.

I've never really understood the interviewer who thinks telling the story of his or her life is pertinent. Why do some interviewers do it? Part nervousness, part inexperience, but mostly because they have the mistaken notion they have to sell *you* on the company, rather than the other way around. There *are* occasions when this *may* be necessary—periods of low unemployment, a glut of particular jobs and a dearth of qualified candidates, a candidate who's so desirable the interviewer feels, perhaps correctly, that he or she has to outsell and outbid the competition.

Under most circumstances, as I instruct novice interviewers in *Ask the Right Questions, Hire the Right People* (this book from the other side of the desk), *you* should be expected to carry the conversational load, while the interviewer sits back and decides if he or she is ready to buy what you're selling.

Is it to your benefit to find yourself seated before Mr. Monologue? You might think so. After all, while he's waxing poetic about the new cafeteria, you don't have to worry about inserting your other foot in your mouth. No explaining that last firing or why you've had four jobs in three months. Nope, just sit back, relax, and try to stay awake.

But I don't believe Mr. M. is doing you any favors. Someone who monopolizes the conversation doesn't give you the opportunity *you* need to "strut your stuff." You may want to avoid leaving a bad impression, but I doubt you want to leave *no* impression at all. As long as you follow the advice in this book and, especially, this chapter, you should welcome the savvy interviewer who asks the open-ended, probing questions *he* needs to identify the right person for the job—the same questions *you* need to convince him it's *you*.

THE "OUT OF IT" INTERVIEWER

Yes, interviewers have been known to be drunk, stoned, or otherwise incapacitated. Some have spent virtually the entire time allotted to a candidate speaking on the phone or browsing e-mail. Others go off on tirades about interoffice disputes or turf wars.

If the interviewer treats you with such apparent indifference before you're even hired, how do you expect him to act once you *are* hired?

There *is* a boss out there willing to treat you with the same respect she would expect from you; it's just not this one. Move on.

TIME TO GET UP CLOSE AND PERSONAL

There are a number of styles and guiding philosophies when it comes to person-to-person interviews. The overall purpose, of course, is to screen you out if you lack the aptitudes (and attitudes) the company is looking for.

Although experienced interviewers may use more than one strategy, it's essential to know which mode you're in at any given point and what to do about it. Here's a summary of the methods and objectives of the most common approaches.

THE BEHAVIORAL INTERVIEW

Your conversations with the interviewer will focus almost exclusively on your past experience as he tries to learn more about how you have already behaved in a variety of on-the-job situations. Then he will attempt to use this information to extrapolate your future reactions on the job.

How did you handle yourself in some really tight spots? What kinds of on-the-job disasters have you survived? Did you do the right thing? What were the repercussions of your decisions?

Be careful what you say. Every situation you faced was unique in its own way, so be sure to let the interviewer in on specific limitations you had to deal with. Did you lack adequate staff or support from management? If you made the mistake of plunging in too quickly, say so and admit that you've learned to think things through. Explain what you'd do differently the next time around.

Remember: Those interviewers using a behavioral interview are trying to ensure you can really walk the walk, not just talk the talk. So leave out the generalizations and philosophizing, and don't get lost in the details. In other words, just tell them the problems you faced, the actions you took, and the results you achieved, without exaggeration.

Which is why composing three or four or more "stories"—actual experiences that illustrate your most important skills or qualifications—is important. Just make sure to structure them in "Problem-Solution-Action" format.

THE TEAM INTERVIEW

Today's organizational hierarchies are becoming flatter. That means that people at every level of a company are more likely to become involved in a variety of projects and tasks, including interviewing *you.*

The team interview can range from a pleasant conversation to a torturous interrogation. Typically, you will meet with a group, or "team," of interviewers around a table in a conference room. They may be members of your prospective department or a cross section of employees from throughout the company. (A slightly less stressful variation is the tag team approach, in which a single questioner exits and is followed by a different questioner a few minutes or questions later.) Rarely will you be informed beforehand to expect a team interview.

The hiring manager or someone from Human Resources may chair an orderly session of question-and-answer; or he may turn the group loose to shoot questions at you like a firing squad. When it's all over, you'll have to survive the assessment of every member of the group.

Some hiring managers consult with the group after the interview for a "reading" on your performance. Others determine their decision using group consensus. The good news is that you don't have to worry that the subjective opinion of just one person will undermine your shot at the job. If one member of the group thinks you lacked confidence or came across as arrogant, others in the group may disagree. The interviewer who leveled the criticism will have to defend her opinion to the satisfaction of the group—or be shot down herself.

A group of people is also more likely (but not guaranteed) to ask you a broader range of questions that may uncover and underline your skills and expertise. Just take your time, and treat every member of the team with the same respect and deference you would the hiring manager.

If you face a series of separate interrogations with a variety of interviewers and are hit with many of the same questions, be sure to vary your answers. Cite different projects, experiences, successes, and even failures. Otherwise, when they meet to compare notes, you'll come off as a "Johnny One Note."

THE STRESS INTERVIEW

Formal qualifications are important, but in some jobs the emotional demands, sudden emergencies, and breakneck pace of work can be downright intimidating, not once in a while, but every day. Even a candidate who knows all the technical moves may wilt under the glare of an etiquette-challenged boss or crumble when inheriting a surrealistically compressed deadline.

When you're interviewing for such a position, whether you're seeking a job as a stockbroker, an air traffic controller, or a prison guard, an interviewer may feel it's almost meaningless to determine if you are capable of performing the job under the *best* conditions. He may well try to assess how you will do under the very *worst* conditions. And that's where the stress interview comes in.

Anyone who's been through one of these never forgets it. A common enough question in this setting could sound gruff or rude, which is exactly how it's supposed to sound. Rather than a pleasant, "So, tell me about yourself," a stress interviewer may snarl (literally), "So, why the hell should I hire *you* for anything?"

How do you know you're facing a stress interview? Here are some techniques an interviewer may use:

- He ridicules everything you say and questions why you're even interviewing at his company.

- He says nothing when you walk into the room . . . and for five minutes afterwards . . . then just stares at you after you answer his first question.

- She keeps you waiting past the scheduled time and then keeps looking at her watch as you answer questions.

- She stares out the window and seems to be completely uninterested in everything you have to say.

- He challenges every answer, disagrees with every opinion, and interrupts you at every turn.

- He doesn't introduce himself when you walk in, just hits you with a tough question.

- She takes phone calls, works on her computer, and/or eats lunch as you interview.

- You may be seated in a broken chair, directly in front of a high-speed fan, or next to an open window . . . in the dead of winter.

I was subjected to a stress interview before I'd ever heard of the technique, which is not the best way to prepare, believe me. (And note that I was *not* applying to be an FBI agent or air traffic controller . . . just a lowly editor!)

Some years ago, I applied for an editorial position at a major publishing company. I made it past the first hurdle, a screening interview conducted in the corporate office. Next, I was invited to come back to meet the director of personnel, Carrie. After greeting me pleasantly, Carrie led me back to her rather palatial office. We chatted for a few minutes as I settled in. Then everything changed. Suddenly, I was undergoing an interrogation worthy of the secret police in a country on Amnesty International's Top Ten List.

Assuming that I had been given good reviews by the screening interviewer, I was shocked when Carrie began firing away. First, she questioned my credentials. Why, she wondered sarcastically, had I majored in liberal arts rather than in something practical? She demanded to know what in the world made me think that I could edit a magazine (even though I had been doing it quite well for years).

Each successive question skittered in a dizzying new direction. If the first question was about my work experience, the next launched into my fitness routine, and the next, my favorite movie.

Carrie's questions did exactly what I later discovered they were intended to do—they made me feel confused, fearful, and hostile. I behaved badly, I admit. I answered most of her questions in monosyllables, avoiding her eyes.

Needless to say, I was not offered the job. But I did learn some valuable lessons from Carrie that day:

- **NEVER LET THEM SEE YOU SWEAT.** No matter how stressful the situation, stay calm. Never take your eyes from the interviewer. When he or she finishes asking a question, take a few seconds to compose yourself and then, and only then, answer.

- **RECOGNIZE THE SITUATION FOR WHAT IT IS—** nothing more than an artificial scenario designed to see how you react under pressure. The interviewer (probably) has nothing against you personally. *It's just a game,* though not a pleasant one for you.

- **DON'T BECOME DESPONDENT.** It's easy to think that the interviewer has taken a strong dislike to you and that your chances for completing the interview process are nil. That's not the case. The stress interview is designed to see if you will become depressed, hostile, or flustered when the going gets tough.

- **WATCH YOUR TONE OF VOICE.** It's easy to become sarcastic during a stress interview, especially if you don't realize what the interviewer is up to.

If you are subjected to a stress interview, you may well question seeking a job with a company that utilizes such techniques. If they think insulting and belittling you during the interview are effective tools, what's their management philosophy—gruel at nine, thumbscrews at two?

Don't confuse a stress interview with a *negative* interview. In the latter, the interviewer merely emphasizes the negative aspects of the job at every opportunity. He may even make some up: "Would you have any problem cleaning the toilets every Saturday morning?" or "Is three hours of daily overtime a problem for you?"

THE CASE INTERVIEW

"You're dealing with a publishing client. His printer just called and said the biggest book of the year had a typo on the spine. A bad typo. More than 100,000 books have already been printed. What should he do?"

There's nothing quite like the terror of the hypothetical question. Especially when it is a product of the interviewer's rich imagination. We'll talk more about these devils in Chapter 7. But for now, know that the hypothetical question should start a red light flashing in your mind. It's your signal that you are about to undergo an increasingly popular type of interview—the case (or situational) interview. If you are seeking a job at a consulting firm, law firm, or counseling organization, you should expect to confront this type of interview.

The premise is sound: Present the candidate with situations that might, hypothetically, occur on the job in order to gauge the degree to which he or she demonstrates the traits that will lead to success. It's hard, if not impossible, for you to prepare for these kinds of questions beforehand, which means you'll have to analyze an unfamiliar problem and develop a strategy to solve it, right then and there.

What most interviewers want to see is a combination of real-world experience, inspired creativity, and the willingness to acknowledge when more information or assistance is in order. (Many interviewers will pose hypothetical questions designed to smoke out people who find it difficult to reach out to other team members for help.) They want to understand how you approach a problem, the framework within which you seek a solution, and the thought process you utilize.

You will have to devote a great deal of thought to each of these questions. If you find yourself caught in this snare, stay calm and use the homework you have done on your personal inventory to untangle yourself.

Here are some tips for confronting a case interview:

- **TAKE NOTES ON THE PROBLEM THAT'S PRESENTED.** Ask questions about the details. Be aware that not all information is pertinent to the solution. (That wily interviewer!)

- **AVOID GENERALIZATIONS.** The interviewer will want to hear concrete steps that will lead to a solution, not your philosophy of how to approach the problem.

- **DON'T GET LOST IN THE DETAILS.** The interviewer wants to see how you approach the broad problem, so set your sights on the most important factors.

- **ASK QUESTIONS.**

- **SHARE YOUR THOUGHTS—OUT LOUD.** That's really what the interviewer wants to hear.

- **RESIST THE URGE FOR SPEED—TAKE YOUR TIME.** The more complicated the problem, the more time you're *expected* to take.

- **THERE'S NOTHING WRONG WITH A CREATIVE AP-PROACH,** but it should always be presented within a logical framework.

While case interviews are geared to upper-echelon candidates, candidates for many different kinds of jobs may be given the opportunity to "walk the walk" (show what they can actually do on the job): Clerks may be given typing or filing tests; copy editors given minutes to edit a magazine article or book chapter; a salesperson may be asked to telephone and sell a prospect; and a computer programmer may be required to create some code. The more technical the job, the more likely an interviewer will not simply take you at your word that you are capable of doing it.

THE BRAINTEASER INTERVIEW

As Microsoft interviewers have famously been known to ask, "How would you move Mt. Fuji?" The list of questions designed to assess how creatively you approach a problem—as opposed to the logical approach case interviews are designed to highlight—are virtually unlimited:

- How many oil wells are there in Texas?

- How many dentists are there in Poland?

- How would you build a better mousetrap?

Most of the same tips I gave you when approaching a case interview are still relevant; take your time, ask pertinent questions, then talk through the approach you would take to answer the question.

In the next chapter, and for the rest of the book, we will explore the hundreds of potential questions you face—and the answers that will help you get the job you want.

HOW TO "ACE" ANY INTERVIEW

● **RELAX!** Think of it as an adventure (as opposed to a tribunal). Try to enjoy yourself. Imagine that the interviewer is a sports star, famous author, or movie celebrity you've always admired. (Try to overlook the middle-aged paunch or glaring bald spot.)

● **KEEP SMILING.** No, not a fake grin. Just maintain a pleasant, relaxed smile that is, hopefully, a by-product of your involvement in an interesting conversation. Put yourself in the interviewer's place. Who wouldn't want to work with such an agreeable person?

● **BE ENTHUSIASTIC.** About the position, your accomplishments, and what you know about the company. But don't gush—if you're not genuinely enthusiastic, you'll come across as a phony.

● **BE HONEST.** Lying about even the smallest or least important details could be grounds for immediate departure.

● **MAKE LOTS OF EYE CONTACT.** Have you ever known someone who wouldn't look you in the eye? After a while, you probably started to wonder what that person had to hide. You don't want your interviewer wondering anything of the sort. So meet his or her eyes while you're shaking hands, then frequently throughout the interview. But don't stare—unrelenting eye contact is as bad as none at all.

● **REMAIN POSITIVE.** As we'll see when we discuss questions about your previous jobs, you must learn to put a positive spin on *everything,* but especially loaded issues, such as your reason for leaving a job, troubled relations with your superiors, or the lack of required qualifications.

● **DON'T LET AN UNSKILLED INTERVIEWER TRIP YOU UP.** Make sure the preparation you've spent so much time on comes shining through, especially when a manager throws you a curve. If need be, your advance preparation should give you the power to take control of the interview, allowing you to emphasize the many ways in which you will benefit the prospective employer.

3

So, Tell Me About Yourself

There it is. The granddaddy of all interview questions. And one that still, unbelievably, makes some of you stumble.

It's really more of a request than a question, but it can put you on the spot like no question can. And if you're unprepared for such an open-ended prelude to the series of standard questions about your skills, background, and aspirations you've been expecting, it can stop you dead and earn you an immediate one-way ticket out of the interview.

Why is this question a favorite of so many interviewers? Many consider it a nice ice-breaker, giving them a chance to gauge initial chemistry, get a little insight into the cipher sitting before them (that would be you), and force *you* to do all the talking, for at least a couple of minutes!

Should this time-tested question catch you unprepared? Certainly not. I guarantee that this will be one of the first three questions asked, often the very first one! So what happens if you do hem and haw your way through a disjointed, free-associating discourse that starts somewhere in Mrs. Mahamita's kindergarten class and, 10 minutes later, is just getting into the details of those 8th grade cheerleader tryouts? You may well tie the record for the shortest interview of the week.

Is the interviewer seeking specific clues (key words, body language)? Or, as I have secretly suspected of many an unseasoned interviewer, is she simply looking for the easiest way to get the ball rolling?

It shouldn't matter to you. If you are prepared, you know this can be your golden opportunity to provide an answer that demonstrates four of the traits every interviewer is desperately searching for: intelligence, enthusiasm, confidence, and dependability.

So dig out the personal inventory you completed in Chapter 1 (I told you it would be an important prerequisite for making good use of this book) and study the items you listed under these headings:

- My strongest skills.

- My greatest areas of knowledge.

- My greatest personality strengths.

- The things I do best.

- My key accomplishments.

WHAT DO THEY WANT TO HEAR?

From this information, you will now construct a well-thought-out, logically sequenced summary of your experience, skills, talents, and schooling. It's a decided plus if this brief introduction clearly and succinctly ties your experience into the requirements of the position. But be sure to keep it tightly focused—about 250 to 350 words, chock-full of specifics. It should take you no more than two minutes to recite an answer that features the following information:

- Brief introduction.

- Key accomplishments.

- Key strengths demonstrated by these accomplishments.

- Importance of these strengths and accomplishments to the prospective employer.

- Where and how you see yourself developing in the position for which you're applying (tempered with the right amount of self-deprecating humor and modesty).

Again, we're not talking *War and Peace* here. Anywhere from 250 to 350 words is about right (taking from 90 to 120 seconds to recite).

 GREEN LIGHT

Here's how Barb, a recent college graduate applying for an entry-level sales position, answered this question:

> *"I've always been able to get along with different types of people. I think it's because I'm a good talker and an even better listener.* [Modestly introduces herself, while immediately laying claim to the most important skills a good salesperson should have.]

> *"During my senior year in high school, when I began thinking seriously about which careers I'd be best suited for, sales came to mind almost immediately. In high school and during my summer breaks from college, I worked various part-time jobs at*

retail outlets. [Demonstrates industriousness and at least some related experience.] *Unlike most of my friends, I actually liked dealing with the public.* [Conveys enthusiasm for selling.]

"However, I also realized that retail had its limitations, so I went on to read about other types of sales positions. I was particularly fascinated by what is usually described as 'consultive selling.' I like the idea of going to a client you have really done your homework on and showing him how your products can help him solve one of his nagging problems, and then following through on that. [Shows interest and enthusiasm for the job.]

"After I wrote a term paper on consultive selling in my senior year of college, I started looking for companies at which I could learn and refine the skills shared by people who are working as account executives. [Shows initiative both in researching the area of consultive selling to write a term paper and in then researching prospective companies.]

"That led me to your company, Mr. Sheldon. I find the prospect of working with companies to increase the energy efficiency of their installations exciting. I've also learned some things about your sales training programs. They sound like they're on the cutting edge. [Gives evidence that she is an enthusiastic self-starter.]

"I guess the only thing I find a little daunting about the prospect of working at Co-generation, Inc., is selling that highly technical equipment without a degree in engineering. By the way, what sort of support does your technical staff lend to the sales effort?" [Demonstrates that she is willing to

learn what she doesn't know and closes by defer-
ring to the interviewer's authority. By asking a
question the interviewer must answer, Barb has also
given herself a little breather. Now the conversational ball sits squarely in the interviewer's court.]

Based on the apparent sincerity and detail of her answers, it's
not a bad little speech of a mere 253 words, is it?

Following is another good example from a more experienced interviewee. With nearly a decade of experience in his
field, Ken is applying for his dream job as a district general manager for a firm that provides maintenance services to commer-
cial and residential properties.

Going in to the interview, he knows he has a couple of
strikes against him. First of all, he's already held four jobs, so he's
moved around a bit. And he doesn't yet have the management
experience required by the job, virtually the equivalent of running a business with revenues of $7 million a year.

But because he has anticipated what might otherwise have
been a devastating first interview question—"Tell me something
that will help me get a better feel for you than what I see here
on the resume" (a slightly aggressive variation on "Tell me about
yourself")—Ken is prepared with this winning counterpunch:

> *"I'm a hard worker who loves this business. I've
> been an asset to the employers I've had, and my ex-
> perience would make me an even greater asset to you.*
>
> *"I think these are the most exciting times that I've
> ever seen in this business. Sure, there's so much more
> competition now, and it's harder than ever to get
> really good help. But all the indications are that
> more and more companies will outsource their
> maintenance needs and that more two-income
> households will require the services that we provide.*

"How do we get a bigger share of this business? How do we recruit and train the best personnel? Because they are, after all, the secret of our success. Those are the key challenges managers face in this industry.

"I can help your company meet those challenges. While resumes don't tell the whole story, mine demonstrates that I'm a hard worker. I've had promotions at every company I've worked for.

"I would bring a good perspective to the position because I've been a doer, as well as a supervisor. The people who have worked for me have always respected my judgment, because they know I have a very good understanding of what they do.

"And I have a terrific business sense. I'm great at controlling expenses. I deploy staff efficiently. I'm fair. And I have a knack for getting along with customers.

"I've always admired your company. I must admit I have adopted some of CleanShine's methods and applied them in the companies I've worked for.

"I see now that you're branching into lawn care. I worked for a landscaping business during my high school summers. How is that business going?"

In a mere 278 words, this successful candidate managed to:

- **FOCUS THE INTERVIEWER ONLY ON THE *POSITIVE* ASPECTS OF HIS RESUME.** Sure, he has changed jobs. But after this answer, the interviewer is likely to think, "Gee, look at what he's managed to accomplish during each step of his career."

- **STEER THE INTERVIEW IN THE DIRECTION *HE* WANTED IT TO GO.** He demonstrated leadership abilities, experience, and a good understanding of the market.

- **INTRODUCE JUST THE RIGHT AMOUNT OF HUMILITY.** While taking every opportunity to turn the spotlight on his many accomplishments and professional strengths, Ken portrayed himself as a "roll-up-the-sleeves" type of manager who will be equally at ease with blue-collar workers and the "suits" back at headquarters.

- **TURN THINGS BACK OVER TO THE INTERVIEWER WITH A VERY INFORMED QUESTION.**

Although both Ken and Barb rehearsed their speeches, neither memorized them word for word. It's important to remember that the interviewer is not asking you to present a perfect essay, just to talk, person to person. Ken also sprinkled in a little industry jargon here and there, which was entirely appropriate.

 RED LIGHT

- **LACK OF EYE CONTACT.** The interviewer is asking this question to find a little rapport, so give her the reaction she's looking for.

- **LACK OF STRONG, POSITIVE PHRASES AND WORDS.** It's the first question and, therefore, your first chance to get off on the right foot. Employ words that convey enthusiasm, responsibility, dedication, and success. If the very first answer is uninspired (especially an answer we all assume has been prepared and even rehearsed), I have almost never seen the interview improve very much.

GETTING READY FOR THE "KILLER QUESTION"

- **COMPLETE YOUR PERSONAL INVENTORY.** If you bypassed the work in Chapter 1, go back and do it now.

- **DISTILL YOUR PERSONAL INVENTORY INTO A COMPELLING OPENING.** Use specifics to paint a short-and-sweet picture of "you," one in which you frame yourself as an enthusiastic and competent professional—the ideal candidate for the job.

- **DON'T MEMORIZE IT WORD FOR WORD.** You want to sound fresh, not like you're reading from a set of internal cue cards. So know the content. Record yourself speaking it until it sounds sincere but spontaneous.

- **INCLUDE STRONG, POSITIVE PHRASES AND WORDS.** You want to convey enthusiasm and confidence as well as knowledge and experience. What you don't know, you're eager to learn.

- **USE IT TO SET THE COURSE OF THE INTERVIEW.** Anticipate that the killer question will surface early in the interview, so be prepared to use it as an opportunity to steer the interview in the direction *you* want it to take. Fine-tune your response to give a positive slant to any potential negatives, such as apparent job-hopping or lack of related experience. Think about particular skills or accomplishments you want to showcase during that interview and prepare at least one good example of each.

- **END WITH THE BALL IN THE INTERVIEWER'S COURT.** By ending with a question, you get a much-deserved breather and, once again, demonstrate your involvement and enthusiasm.

Many interviewers will simply cut their losses and move on to a more promising candidate.

● **A GENERAL, MEANDERING RESPONSE THAT FAILS TO CITE/HIGHLIGHT SPECIFIC ACCOMPLISHMENTS.** It's a plus if you have been savvy enough to edit what we all know is a well-rehearsed set speech to ensure that it's relevant to the job at hand. Many interviewers *will* consider it a minus if all they've heard is a bunch of generalities and few (or no) actual specifics to back them up.

● **NO RELEVANCE TO JOB OR COMPANY.** The interviewer did *not* ask you to tell her about your hobbies, dog, and favorite ice cream flavor or boy band. Some interviewers may give you the initial benefit of the doubt if your answer is too general or personal, but most will quickly probe for some job-related specifics.

● **LACK OF ENTHUSIASM.** If you don't seem excited about interviewing for the job, most interviewers will not assume you'll suddenly "get religion" once you're hired.

● **NERVOUSNESS.** Some people are naturally nervous in the artificial and intimidating atmosphere of an interview, and most experienced interviewers won't consider this an automatic reason to have their secretary buzz them about that "emergency conference." But they'll wonder what may be lurking—a firing, a sexual harassment suit, *some*thing that isn't going to make their day.

● **SOMEONE WHO ASKS A CLARIFYING QUESTION,** such as "What exactly do you want to know?"

or "Which particular areas would you like me to talk about?" As I said earlier, I find it hard to believe anyone interviewing for anything has not anticipated that this question will be asked. What do you *think* the interviewer wants to know? Your opinion about the 2006 midterm elections? She wants to know about your experience, skills, talents, and education, so answer the question, articulately and succinctly, and get ready for what comes next.

VARIATIONS

- *What makes you special (unique, different)?*

- *What five adjectives describe you best?*

- *Rate yourself on a scale of 1 to 10.*

- *How would you describe your character?*

- *How would you describe your personality?*

Despite the nuances, you should merely edit your "set piece" to respond to each of the above questions in essentially the same way. So although the first, fourth, and fifth questions appear to be more targeted, all five are really looking for the same information.

- *Why should I hire you?*

- *Why should I consider you a strong candidate for this position?*

- *What's better about you than the other candidates I'm interviewing?*

- *What can you do for us that someone else can't?*

These are more aggressive questions, the tone of each a bit more forceful. An interviewer using one of these variations is clearly attempting to make you fully aware that you're on the hot seat. This may be a matter of his particular style, the introduction to his own brand of stress interview, or just a way to save time by seeing how you respond to pressure right from the get-go.

The interviewer has set you up, trying to separate the "misqualified" by using a single question. But he has actually given you a golden opportunity to display the extent of your preinterview research. And if you haven't *done* any, you may well find yourself in a sea of hot water.

 ## WHAT ARE YOUR STRENGTHS AS AN EMPLOYEE?

 ## WHAT DO THEY WANT TO HEAR?

To prepare for this question (as well as the variations just mentioned), pull out those Data Input Sheets you labored over in Chapter 1 and write down the description of the position for which you're interviewing. This will help you clarify each specific job requirement in your mind. Then, match your strengths and accomplishments directly to the requirements of the job.

Let's presume you have a singular skill for meeting even the most unreasonable deadlines. You are tenacious. Nothing can stop you. If meeting deadlines is a key job requirement, be sure to cite two or three pertinent examples from your experience. The more outrageous the deadline and Herculean your efforts, the more important it is to bring to the interviewer's attention—at least twice.

Are there any gaps in your qualifications? Probably a few, especially if you're reaching for the challenge at the next level of your career. So now it's time to dig in and deal with the hard questions that you know will follow the ones above.

HOW WOULD YOUR BEST FRIEND (COLLEGE ROOMMATE, FAVORITE PROFESSOR, FAVORITE BOSS, MOTHER, FAMILY, ETC.) DESCRIBE YOU?

 WHAT DO THEY WANT TO HEAR?

Personally, I would start with the "best friend" variation if I were interviewing someone. Supposedly, that's who should know you best. So if you presented me with a half-baked picture of yourself, I'd shorten the interview—by about seven-eighths of an hour. Another approach some interviewers prefer is to ask you to describe your best friend and how you differ from each other. This is based on the untested but reasonable theory that if someone is your best friend, the two of you probably have quite a lot in common. Because you are supposedly describing your best friend, not yourself, some interviewers believe you may inadvertently reveal character insights (read: flaws) you would otherwise like to conceal. So take pains to describe a person the interviewer would find easy to hire.

All of the other variations on this question may be used by experienced interviewers to hone in on specific times (college, high school, last job) or just to get a fuller picture of you. What your mother or father would say, for example, may give the interviewer a clear illustration of the kind of environment in which you were raised.

 WHAT DO YOU WANT TO BE DOING FIVE YEARS FROM NOW?

 WHAT DO THEY WANT TO HEAR?

Are the company's goals and yours compatible? Are you looking for fast or steady growth in a position the interviewer knows is a virtual dead end? Are you requesting more money than he can ever pay? How have your goals and motivations changed as you have matured and gained work experience? If you've recently become a manager, how has that promotion affected your future career outlook? If you've realized you need to acquire or hone a particular skill, how and when are you planning to do so?

This question is not as popular as it once was, since the pace of change at many corporations continues to increase so rapidly. You are more likely to be asked to concentrate on a much tighter time frame: "What will you be able to accomplish during your first 90 (100, 180) days on the job?"

 ## GREEN LIGHT

Naturally, you want a position of responsibility in your field. But you don't want to give the impression that you're a piranha waiting to feed on the guppies in your new department. So, start humbly:

> *"Well, that will ultimately depend on my perfor-mance on the job and on the growth and opportu-nities offered by my employer."*

Then toot your own horn a bit:

> *"I've already demonstrated leadership characteris-tics in all of the jobs I've held, so I'm very confident that I will take on progressively greater management responsibilities in the future. That suits me fine. I enjoy building a team, developing its goals, and then working to accomplish them. It's very rewarding."*

In other words, you want "more"—more responsibility, more people reporting to you, more turf, even more money. A general answer (as above) is okay, but don't be surprised when an interviewer asks the obvious follow-up questions (using the answer to the above question as a guide):

"Tell me about the last team you led."

"Tell me about the last project your team undertook."

"What was the most satisfying position you've held, and why?"

"If I told you our growth was phenomenal and you could go as far as your abilities would take you, where would that be, and how quickly?"

 RED LIGHT

If you answer, "Your job." Hasn't *everyone* tired of that trite response by now?

If you refuse to offer more than a general answer (that is, no real specific goals, no matter how hard the interviewer probes for more). Your inability or unwillingness to cite specific, positive goals may give the impression, warranted or not, that you have not taken the time to really think about your future, which makes it impossible for the interviewer to assess whether there's a good fit between his goals and yours.

If you insist you want to be in the same job for which you're applying (unless it is a dead-end job and the interviewer would be pleased as punch if someone actually stayed longer than three weeks, unlike the last 14 people to hold the position!).

Any answer that reveals unrealistic expectations. A savvy candidate should have some idea of the time it takes to climb the career ladder in a particular industry or even in a particular company. Someone hoping to go from receptionist to CEO in two years will, of course, scare off most interviewers, but *any* expectations that are far too ambitious could give them pause. If a law school grad, for example, seeks to make partner in 4 years (when the average for all firms is 7 and, for this one, 10), it will make even novice interviewers question the extent and effectiveness of your preinterview research.

There's nothing wrong with being ambitious and confident beyond all bounds, but a savvy interviewee should temper such boundless expectations during the interview. Most interviewers are aware that some candidates do break the rules successfully, but they will get a little nervous around people exhibiting unbridled ambition!

If you have made an interviewer worry that her company couldn't possibly deliver on the promises you seem to want to hear, you can expect a follow-up question: "How soon after you're hired do you think you can contribute to our success?" Even someone with a tremendous amount of appropriate experience knows full well that each company has its own particular ways of doing things and that the learning curve may be days, weeks, or months, depending on the circumstances. So any candidate—but especially an overly ambitious young person—who blithely assures an interviewer they'll be productive from Day One is cause for concern. The interviewer is really trying to assess, in the case of an inexperienced person, how trainable you are, and you've just told him you think you already know it all! Not a good start.

For some reason, some applicants fail to remember that this is an interview, not a conversation in a bar or with friends. As a result, they rattle off some remarkable responses that can only be deemed fantasies—to be retired, own their own business, etc.— though why they would think this is an answer relevant to their job search is beyond me. I would seriously discourage ever answering this question in such a manner.

VARIATIONS

- *What are your most important long-term goals?*
- *Have you recently established any new objectives or goals?*
- *What do you want to do with your life?*

These questions provide you with an opportunity to demonstrate how your goals and motivations have changed as you've matured and gained valuable work experience. If you've recently become a manager, talk about how that experience has affected your career outlook for the future. If you've realized that you must sharpen a particular skill to continue growing, tell the interviewer what you're doing about it.

 IF YOU COULD CHANGE ONE THING ABOUT YOUR PERSONALITY JUST BY SNAPPING YOUR FINGERS, WHAT WOULD IT BE AND WHY?

 WHAT DO THEY WANT TO HEAR?

That you have weaknesses (of course you do!) but none that are lethal. Conventional career advice has been to cite a weakness that you can easily show is really a strength: "You know, sir, I just work too hard. I have to take more time off than just Sunday from 5 to 7." Sure you do.

An answer most interviewers would fine acceptable would reveal a weakness *that you've already corrected* or, in a slight redirection of the question, a mistake you made in a previous job and the lesson(s) you learned from it. In both cases, you would be turning a negative question into a positive response.

My strategy was always to cite a particular skill or qualification that I obviously lacked . . . but one that wasn't remotely needed in the job I was interviewing for.

 RED LIGHT

Identifying a weakness that is job-related or, worse, essential to the job at hand (for example, the inability to work with others when the job at hand is highly team-based).

Citing a weakness that is so basic or stupid that the interviewer has to wonder if that's the *biggest* thing (she *did* say *one* thing) you could change.

VARIATIONS

- *Tell me about the one thing in your life you're proudest of.*

- *Tell me about the worst decision you ever made.*

- *Tell me about the one thing in your life you're most ashamed of.*

- *What's your greatest weakness?*

The first puts you on comfortable turf—a positive question you can answer positively. The latter three questions force you to turn a negative question into a positive answer, and, because any negative question invites the unwary to descend into a sea of recriminations ("Working for that last jerk, let me tell you!"), it is a potential quagmire.

In all cases, the interviewer is inviting conversation but not as "one way" and open-ended as in earlier questions. These might well be follow-up questions if "Tell me about yourself" or a similar question didn't open everything up as much as the interviewer hoped they would. You should, therefore, take them as a sign that you've yet to tell the interviewer what he wants to hear.

 DESCRIBE YOUR MANAGEMENT PHILOSOPHY.

 WHAT DO THEY WANT TO HEAR?

Most companies want someone who can demonstrate a desire and ability to delegate, teach, and distribute work—and credit—fairly (unless, of course, the interviewer is an autocratic jerk seeking a mirror image). In general, you probably want to come across as neither a dictator nor a pushover. Successful candidates should convey that they have the ability to succeed should opportunity present itself. But they should avoid giving the impression that they're fire-breathing workaholics ready to succeed no matter what (or whom) the cost.

 GREEN LIGHT

> *"More than anything else, I think that manage-*
> *ment is getting things done through other people.*
> *The manager's job is to provide the resources and*
> *environment in which people can work effectively.*
> *I try to do this by creating teams, judging people*
> *solely on the basis of their performance, distributing*
> *work fairly, and empowering workers, to the extent*
> *possible, to make their own decisions. I've found*
> *that this breeds loyalty and inspires hard work."*

 RED LIGHT

One of these wishy-washy answers I've actually heard during interviews:

> *"I try to get people to like me, and then they really*
> *work hard for me." "I guess you could say I'm a*
> *real people-person."*

 WHAT DOES SUCCESS MEAN TO YOU?

 WHAT DO THEY WANT TO HEAR?

You should offer a balanced answer to this question, citing personal as well as professional examples. If your successes are exclusively job-related, an interviewer may wonder if you actually have a life. However, if you blather on about your personal goals and accomplishments, you may seem uncommitted to striving for success on the job.

GREEN LIGHT

Strike a balance and talk about success in terms such as these:

"I have always enjoyed supervising a design team. In fact, I've discovered that I'm better at working with other designers than designing everything myself. Unlike a lot of the people in my field, I'm also able to relate to the requirements of the manufacturing department.

"So, I guess I'd say success means working with others to come up with efficient designs that can be up on the assembly line quickly. Of course, the financial rewards of managing a department give me the means to travel during my vacations. That's the thing I love most in my personal life."

RED LIGHT

If the interviewer identifies any of the following problems from your answer, you're already on thin ice and better get back to shore:

- Incompatibility between his/her goals and yours.

- Lack of focus in your answer.

- Too general an answer, with no examples of what success has already been achieved.

- Too many personal examples.

- Too many job-oriented examples.

WHAT DOES FAILURE MEAN TO YOU?

 WHAT DO THEY WANT TO HEAR?

A specific example to demonstrate what *you* mean by failure, *not* a lengthy philosophical discussion more suited to a Bergman film than an interview. This question offers an experienced interviewer the opportunity to delve into mistakes and bad decisions—not a happy topic as far as you're concerned. He is looking for honesty, a clear analysis of what went wrong, a willingness to admit responsibility (with a small plus if it's obvious you're taking responsibility for some aspects that *weren't* your fault), and evidence that you are determined to change what caused it (or examples to show how it's already been transformed).

 GREEN LIGHT

> *"Failure is not getting the job done when I have the means to do so. For example, once I was faced with a huge project. I should have realized at the outset that I didn't have the time. I must have been thinking there were 48 hours in a day! I also didn't have the knowledge I needed to do it correctly. Instead of asking some of the other people in my department for help, I blundered through. That won't ever happen to me again if I can help it!"*

 RED LIGHT

A wishy-washy, nonspecific answer that forces the interviewer to ask more and more follow-up questions to get some sort of handle on what makes you tick.

Always remember why the interviewer is asking you such open-ended questions: to get you talking, hopefully so you reveal more than you would have if he or she had asked a more pointed question. So answer such questions—clearly, succinctly, and specifically—but avoid any temptation to confess your many sins.

VARIATIONS

- *What does "achievement" mean to you?*

- *What does "challenge" mean to you?*

- *What does "problem" mean to you?*

- *What does "impossible" mean to you?*

- *What does "growth" mean to you?*

TIPS FOR CONVINCING THE INTERVIEWER YOU'RE A GREAT CATCH

- **DO YOUR HOMEWORK.** Find out as much as you can about the company and how the position for which you're interviewing contributes to its goals.

- **DEMONSTRATE EXPERIENCE AND EXUDE CONFIDENCE.** Give the interviewer strong answers using concrete examples that are relevant to the position you are after.

- **BE HUMBLE.** Convey the impression that you have the ability to succeed should opportunities present themselves. But avoid giving the impression that you're a fire-breathing workaholic ready to succeed no matter what (or whom) the cost.

- **APPEAR FIRM, BUT NOT DICTATORIAL.** When you talk about your management philosophy, let the interviewer know that you are able to delegate, keep track of each person's progress, and stay on top of your own work.

- **TALK ABOUT GROWTH.** Tell the interviewer how you've grown in each of the jobs you've held and how your career goals have changed as a result.

- **ADMIT TO YOUR FAILURES.** Concentrate on what you learned from past failures, using examples that show how you've changed as a result of them.

- **SHOWCASE YOUR SUCCESSES.** Make sure to position yourself as a professional with a satisfying personal life.

Why Did You Major in Astrophysics and Minor in Theater?

The more work experience you have, the less anyone will care about what you did in college, even if you attended Podunk rather than Princeton. As important as particular courses and extracurricular leadership positions may have been a decade ago, no amount of educational success can take the place of solid, real-world, on-the-job experience.

But if your diploma is so fresh the ink could stain your fingers and your only (summer) job was intimately involved with salad ingredients, then the questions in this chapter are directed to you, the relatively inexperienced candidate facing that age-old Catch-22: You need experience to get the job, but how can you get experience if you can't get a job?

So it's back to Creative Thinking 101. On your resume and in your interviews, you'll attempt to upgrade your experience, no matter how little or minor, while avoiding the temptation to blatantly transform a summer job at the local hot dog stand or on the beach into what sounds like a divisional vice presidency.

How are you going to accomplish this? By concentrating on what the interviewer wants to hear and making sure you give it to him or her. You want to portray yourself as a well-rounded person who, in addition to getting decent grades, demonstrated desirable traits—leadership, team-building, writing, communicating—either through extracurricular activities, internships, and/or part-time work experience. If you weren't a member of many official school clubs or teams, talk about other activities you engaged in during college. Did you work part-time? Tutor other students? Work for extra course credit?

Don't list just a major and minor on your resume; include pertinent courses, too. And a truly savvy candidate will ensure that each resume is custom-produced so the particular courses mesh as closely as possible with the requirements of the job.

What you've been doing—*whatever* you have been doing—should demonstrate a pattern that bears at least some passing relation to the job at hand. What you did during your summers, unless it was a pertinent internship or part-time job, is virtually irrelevant. You *chose* a major, courses, activities; most interviewers will want to know the reasons why you made *those particular choices.* That will reveal to them where your real interests lie . . . no matter what perfect "objective" you've branded onto your resume.

 WHAT EXTRACURRICULAR ACTIVITIES WERE YOU INVOLVED IN?

 WHAT DO THEY WANT TO HEAR?

Most interviewers are seeking a candidate who can illustrate industriousness, not just someone who did enough to eke by.

They're expecting enthusiasm, confidence, energy, dependability, honesty, a problem solver, a team player, someone who's willing to work hard to achieve difficult but worthy goals.

 ## GREEN LIGHT

Activities that bear some relationship to the job/industry (for example, a college newspaper editor applying for a job in newspaper, book, or magazine publishing).

Activities that show a healthy balance. You are probably a top candidate for a wide variety of jobs if you participated in one or more sports *and* a cultural club (chess, theater, etc.) *and* a political club *and* you worked part-time, as opposed to someone whose sole focus was on a sport or cause, no matter how illustrious his or her athletic or other achievements.

If you're able to demonstrate the ability to manage multiple priorities (let's not forget coursework and maybe a part-time job here) and good time-management skills. Here's a good answer:

> *"I wish I'd had more time to write for the school paper. Whenever I wasn't studying, I pretty much had to work to pay for college. But I learned a number of things from the jobs I held that most people learn only after they've been in their careers for a while, such as how to work with other people and how to manage my time effectively."*

 ## RED LIGHT

If you've spent an inordinate amount of time doing things outside of class but your GPA (Grade Point Average) indicates you spent too *little* time concentrating *in* class. (Anything below a B average should lead you to expect a whole series of follow-up questions forcing you to explain why your grades weren't better.)

If you have seemingly tried every activity at least once and have demonstrated no clear direction, most interviewers will not assume you'll suddenly change on the job.

Never presume a joke is a good answer: "Well, Mr. Johns, I didn't do much more than drink beer on weekends." I'm probably more appreciative of good jokes than the next guy, but an interview is simply the wrong place and the wrong time to channel Letterman. Even if you're funny, most interviewers will probably question the common sense of anyone who thinks sitting across from their desk applying for a job is a good time and place to test a new stand-up routine.

VARIATIONS

- *What made you choose those activities?*

- *Which ones did you most enjoy? Why?*

- *Which ones did you least enjoy? Why?*

- *Which ones do you regret not choosing? Why?*

The interviewer posing questions like these is just trying to get a handle on how you think, how you make choices and decisions, and how flexible or inflexible you seem to be in those choices.

 WHY DID YOU CHOOSE YOUR COLLEGE? WHY DID YOU CHOOSE YOUR MAJOR? WHY DID YOU CHOOSE YOUR MINOR? WHICH COURSES DID YOU LIKE MOST? WHICH DID YOU LIKE LEAST?

 WHAT DO THEY WANT TO HEAR?

Some interviewers may substitute this series of questions for the ubiquitous "So, tell me about yourself"—your college experience is probably a good measure of "yourself."

If you were a liberal arts major, talk about the skills you developed in some of your courses: writing ability; researching and analytical skills; debating, language and communication skills. Assuming that you took courses related to the job at hand, focus only on those that are career-oriented.

Don't feel handicapped if you majored in something nontechnical or nonprofessional. Most interviewers, even those offering fairly technical jobs, expect to spend an inordinate amount of their time cajoling an endless line of History, English, and French Lit majors to explain how their college education prepared them for a sales/marketing/management/executive position.

What was your thought process? Did you choose a major because it was the easiest? Because it had specific relevance to other interests (as demonstrated by consistent volunteer/work/activities)? Because you analyzed the job market and took courses to prepare for a particular career/industry? Just because it was there?

What other majors or minors did you consider? And why did you choose one and reject the others?

If you are being interviewed for a highly technical job—engineering, science, programming, and the like—the interviewer should reasonably expect that you majored in engineering, chemistry, or computer science, and that your major and even minor coursework is pertinent (with the exception of someone like my friend Andy, who majored in Astrophysics at MIT . . . and minored in Theater). It will probably be a plus if you demonstrated a particular interest in chemistry or computers or mechanical engineering while still in high school.

 ## GREEN LIGHT

Talk about the skills you developed, especially in courses you didn't necessarily like or want to take. I *like* to hear that a candidate did well in a course she really didn't care for. I seem to spend an inordinate amount of time doing things *I* don't care for, but I still must do them to the best of my ability. When I interview people, I guarantee you I'm seeking someone with the same attitude.

When talking about particular courses, develop answers that focus on the subject, *not* the workload or the professor's personality. Talking about past troubles with an authority figure will introduce a possible negative into your current candidacy. And complaining about too much work is not the best way to impress any prospective boss.

Interviewers don't take kindly to freshly minted graduates who expect to start at a salary higher than their own. So acknowledge that you are well aware that despite your *summa cum laude* credentials, you probably have less job-related knowledge than the senior person in the mailroom. Humility is an attractive trait at times, especially when it's well deserved: "I know this position has its share of unpleasant duties, but I'm sure everyone who's had this job before me has learned a lot by doing them."

 RED LIGHT

Blaming a professor, even tangentially, for a bad grade or experience will give many interviewers pause—do you have problems with authority figures?

Complaining about the workload of a course, semester, or year. Interviewers are seeking industriousness, not laziness.

There are interviewers out there (and I'm one of them) who go out of their way to describe in excruciating detail the worst or most mind-numbingly boring aspects of the job. A successful candidate shouldn't be fooled into expressing *any* negative reaction (even a raised eyebrow when "garbage detail" is being discussed!).

VARIATIONS

● *Why did you change majors? Change minors? Drop that course? Add that course?*

WHAT DO THEY WANT TO HEAR?

Again, what was the thought process? The change may well be considered a positive—if you explain and justify it well—unless, of course, it clearly was to eliminate a difficult major for an easier one, a stratagem to take more classes with a girlfriend, or something equally superfluous.

If you have changed majors, even more than once, you must be ready to admit that you simply didn't have all the answers when you were 19. (Don't worry, neither did the interviewer.) I suspect many interviewers would find such candor refreshing and realistic. After all, how many high school seniors know that eventually they will (or want to) become accountants, hospital administrators, loading dock foremen, or, for that matter, interviewers? But you should be prepared to show how your other studies contributed to making you the best candidate for the job.

 WHY ARE YOU APPLYING FOR A JOB IN A FIELD OTHER THAN YOUR MAJOR?

 WHAT DO THEY WANT TO HEAR?

Life doesn't always turn out according to our plans. Especially when we're young, changes in direction are common. Changes are hard enough to live through without getting grilled about them. But when the interviewer asks about one of your 180-degree turns, you've got to respond.

If you're applying for a retail management position and your degree is in geology, there's a good chance that you'll be asked this question; it's not the first time this employer has encountered someone like you. In today's job market, changing careers is common, and there's nothing unique about going into a field other than the one you majored in.

So what do you do? You know you've piqued the employer's interest enough to get an interview, right? So relax and answer the question. Keep it brief and positive: You've reexamined your career goals. You enjoy customer contact, the competitive nature of sales, and the varied management responsibilities required in retail, and you've decided it's the career you want to pursue. And, oh yeah (perhaps with a sheepish grin), there are only 142 new jobs in geology this year, and you didn't get any of them!

Then it may be a good idea to pause and ask, "Have I answered your question?" Give the interviewer an opportunity to express concerns about your qualifications. If he has any, be prepared to explain how the skills required in your degree field transfer to the field in which you're seeking employment. You can use the same strategy with your prior work experience. Are there particular things a geologist must learn that directly translate into retail management? Particular skills? *I* don't know, but *you* certainly better be ready to talk about them.

Just because many students who major in more esoteric areas are, by definition, ill-prepared for some specific jobs, and just because many people now change jobs, careers, and even industries more and more, does *not* mean that many interviewers will not make you sell them on how your learning will benefit *them*.

 IF YOU WERE STARTING COLLEGE TOMORROW, WHAT COURSES WOULD YOU TAKE?

 WHAT DO THEY WANT TO HEAR?

Be prepared to detail what you could have changed about your course selections that would have made you a better candidate for this job. Should you have taken more marketing courses, an accounting course, a statistics seminar? At the same time, don't be afraid to admit that it took you a little while to find the right course of study.

A bit of candor is fine, but avoid offering a dissertation involving a wholesale change of major, minor, and hair color.

 ## GREEN LIGHT

Consider this question a good opportunity to describe how courses that are completely unrelated to this or any other real-world career nevertheless were valuable in your development.

 ## RED LIGHT

Don't claim you would have gone away to school so you could date more.

Don't answer, "Same courses, but this time I'd pass."

Don't answer in a way that clearly implies you don't understand the purpose of the question. You have been given an opportunity to show you know what the job entails and, because of that understanding, to declare you would have taken more pertinent courses while dropping that 17th-century Chinese literature course like a hot chopstick.

 ## WHAT DID YOU LEARN FROM THE INTERNSHIPS ON YOUR RESUME?

 ## WHAT DO THEY WANT TO HEAR?

No company really believes that you're going to hit the ground running right out of college or graduate school. Training and experience will be necessary to make you productive. So, as a relatively inexperienced candidate, you can expect an interviewer to do a bit of probing, trying to determine how trainable you are.

Stress how the real-world internship experience you've had complemented your academic training. But never pretend that college is where you learned the "secret of life." No interviewer is going to react favorably to someone who acts like he or she already knows it all.

GREEN LIGHT

If you are able to show how the internship experience you had complemented your academic training.

Pertinent internships that tie in directly to your new job/career.

Well-thought-out answers that demonstrate consistent career concerns.

Good recommendations from internship supervisors.

RED LIGHT

If you sincerely believe—and, worse, actually tell the interviewer—that college is where you learned the "secret of life."

No internships in a field in which they are *de rigueur.*

An internship in an unrelated field (especially if it ties in with your courses/activities, indicating that your *real* area of interest lies elsewhere).

A poor or no recommendation from your internship supervisor or a negative reaction from you about its value. (Even if your internship turned out to test nothing more than your coffee-making skills, you should *never* introduce such a negative into the interview.)

VARIATIONS

- *Why are there no internships on your resume?*

- *Would you repeat each of your internships?*

- *Why did you pick those particular internships?*

- *Why did you feel the need to do an internship?*

IN WHAT COURSES DID YOU GET THE WORST GRADES? WHY? HOW DO YOU THINK THAT WILL AFFECT YOUR PERFORMANCE ON THIS JOB?

 WHAT DO THEY WANT TO HEAR?

Many companies will ask to see copies of your college transcripts if you don't have work experience. So you might as well spill the beans now!

If you flunked every accounting course, you're probably not applying for an accounting job, right? Hopefully, you can blame the poor grades you received in some of your electives on the amount of time and effort you were putting into your major.

Do interviewers expect that every interviewee is a straight-A student and, therefore, will have a hard time answering this question? Not in my world. So the answer to the first part of the question is less important than the explanation and how you handle introducing a negative: "Yes, sir, I flunked Statistical Analysis, but it was completely outside my major and, as far as I know, has nothing to do with the job you're offering."

 GREEN LIGHT

If you really can't answer the question because you didn't get any bad grades!

If you satisfactorily explain the one or two less-than-stellar grades. If a poor grade was in an elective course, blame the extra time you spent on your major (in which, of course, you did great). If you blew a single major course, perhaps outside activities were to blame (and you have a ready explanation for why you placed such activities ahead of good grades).

RED LIGHT

Too many Cs and Ds to count.

No reasonable explanation, leading an interviewer to assume that you simply didn't care or aren't all that bright.

A choice that you made based on wisdom most interviewers would question. Although it may have been quite exciting and educational to devote a significant amount of time to getting your friend elected Student Body President, were a plethora of Ds a viable trade-off?

VARIATIONS

- *Are grades a good measure of ability?*

- *Why didn't you get better grades?*

- *Why are your grades so erratic?*

- *What happened that semester (year) when your grades sunk?*

 WHAT DO THEY WANT TO HEAR?

Again, if your grades were great, you should be suitably proud; if they weren't, hopefully there were mitigating circumstances: work, an unusual opportunity, a family crisis, whatever. But if you fail to take responsibility for a poor performance, most interviewers will consider it a big red light. Whatever you do, don't become defensive. This will lead most interviewers to wonder whether you actually made a choice or simply did something without thinking of the consequences.

SPECIAL TIPS FOR RECENT COLLEGE GRADS

○ Don't be afraid to say you'll need help. And when you do need help, make sure that the interviewer knows you'll ask for it. Not many companies are looking for, or expect to find, a 22-year-old know-it-all. If you *are* a 22-year-old know-it-all, keep it to yourself.

○ Admit that you don't have all the answers. Or begin a lot of your answers with "I think . . ." or "From what I know about the industry. . . ."

○ Don't appear squeamish at the idea of going through the school of hard knocks. Tell the interviewer, "Sure, I know this position has its share of unpleasant duties, but I'm sure everyone who's had this job before me has learned a lot by doing them."

○ If it took awhile for you to find your direction, admit it. Nobody has all the answers at 18 or 19. Most interviewers will not be surprised that you changed your major as an undergraduate. Show how your other studies contributed to making you the best candidate.

○ Don't answer any question about who paid for your educational expenses or about any outstanding educational loans you may be carrying. Go ahead and play up the fact that you received a full academic scholarship or were industrious enough to work your way through school, if you want to. But by law, you don't have to say any more. For more detail on how to recognize and deflect illegal questions, see Chapter 9.

Are You Experienced?

t should come as no surprise that most interview questions will focus on your previous work experience. You've bid your alma mater adieu, either last decade or last week, so what have you done out there in the real world? Many employers think that your past is a prologue to your future performance. If you do have some deep, dark character flaw, they figure it must have shown up already!

So be prepared to be thoroughly grilled about every job you've ever had, especially the last two or three. And stay positive through it all.

Let's look at some of the questions you're likely to field.

TELL ME ABOUT YOUR LAST THREE POSITIONS. EXPLAIN WHAT YOU DID, HOW YOU DID IT, THE PEOPLE YOU WORKED FOR, AND THE PEOPLE YOU WORKED WITH.

WHAT DO THEY WANT TO HEAR?

Whew! This is a shotgun approach, in part designed to see how well you organize what could be a lot of data into a brief, coherent overview of 3, 5, 10, or more years' experience. Interviewers who ask these questions, or ones like them, are trying to flesh out your resume, catch inconsistencies, create a roadmap for the far more detailed inquiries to follow, and evaluate how well you edit your answers to match your experience and skills to the requirements of the job at hand.

 ## GREEN LIGHT

If you can boast pertinent experience and skills in a brief, coherent, positive answer.

If you are cognizant of the importance of relating *your* experience and skills to *the interviewer's* job requirements.

A clear pattern *upward:* Increased responsibility, authority, money, subordinates, skill level, and so on.

 ## RED LIGHT

Asking the interviewer *my* least favorite question: "What exactly do you want to know?" (Answer: What I just asked for!)

Any answer that is inconsistent with the facts on your resume (dates, duties, titles). You would think no one would refer to a job that doesn't appear on his or her resume, but it happens all the time. (And if you hint at such a problem, here's how a good interviewer will make you sweat: "Your resume says that you were working at _____ during 2002, but you just said you were working at _____. How do you explain that?")

I'll admit to being part of the stupidest interview ever undertaken by an otherwise smart, reasonably experienced person. I spent the first five years after graduating from Princeton trying to be a full-time writer without actually starving to death. The only way to accomplish that was to work a series of short-term, part-time jobs (often two or three at once) while I frantically turned out short stories, newspaper/magazine articles, plays, screenplays, and, eventually, books, some of which I actually got paid for.

How many different jobs did I have? Dozens. Some lasted a day, some months, one nearly two years.

But the only one that appeared on my resume was the two-year stint at a trade association, because my supervisor graciously agreed to back up my white lie and allow me to claim that it was full-time, for five years.

Within 10 minutes of sitting down in front of the interviewer for a major magazine company, I was blithely discoursing on what I had learned at two or three of these other jobs. Yes, that's right, the ones that officially didn't exist. I finally realized what I had done . . . a minute or so after the interviewer. At about the same time, the interviewer and I both tumbled to the reality—I wasn't getting this job or, for that matter, any other potential job at that magazine company. We parted, amiably, though I felt like a small poodle that had been pulled through one too many mud puddles.

So don't torpedo your candidacy by detailing jobs, responsibilities, and skills that don't officially exist. It worked for me!

Don't complain in any way, shape, or form about bosses, subordinates, or coworkers. Most interviewers will fail to be impressed by anyone attempting to blame everyone else for his or her failures. *Even if you weren't at fault,* any transfer of blame will not be deemed a positive.

Most interviewers will grill you about lateral moves (why didn't you get promoted?) and, even more so, clear demotions. You'd better have a very good explanation ready.

 WHAT WAS YOUR FAVORITE JOB? WHY?

 WHAT DO THEY WANT TO HEAR?

The description of the job the interviewer is discussing.

GREEN LIGHT

Presuming that you have to acknowledge that your favorite job differs from the job at hand in a couple of very specific, perhaps even important ways, you can still recover if you can explain why and how you have changed so that the current job is much more appropriate for you *now.*

 RED LIGHT

Any answer that inadvertently reveals the kind of job you're really seeking—obviously *not the one being offered:*

> *"My favorite job was at WNSD radio. It was very loose and informal and there was little supervision, which I really enjoyed. I had the freedom to program my own shows with little or no interference and only had to put in 20 hours a week to actually get my work done, so the rest of the time I could write or think up new creative ideas."*

This sounds like a reasonable answer . . . if only you weren't applying for a job assisting four high-powered businesspeople who are always on deadline and require 10 hours a week overtime at a highly structured and very rigid old-line firm.

It's not a problem if your last job offered some travel and this one doesn't, or if the previous position offered more varied tasks and this one is more highly focused. But it *is* a problem if your answer *fails to take into account what the current job entails,* which will indicate to many interviewers a lack of preinterview research or the simple inability to realize the importance of matching *your* past experience to *their* needs.

TELL ME ABOUT THE BEST/WORST BOSS YOU EVER HAD.

 ## WHAT DO THEY WANT TO HEAR?

Talk about a loaded question! If you're asked to talk about the best boss you ever had, you could try for an on-the-spot description of the hiring manager sitting across the desk from you.

But as a rule of thumb, most companies want to hear that you most enjoyed working for someone who was interested in helping you learn and grow, involved in monitoring your progress, and generous about giving credit where and when it was due. I hope you've had the chance to work for someone like that!

Now, what do you say about your *worst* boss? Don't get carried away with venomous accusations. They may serve only to introduce doubt about your own competence or ability to get along with other people.

For example, if you level the charge of favoritism, the interviewer might wonder why your boss liked other employees more than you. If you complain about a boss who was always looking over your shoulder, the interviewer might wonder whether it was because you couldn't be trusted to complete a task accurately, on budget, on time, or all three.

 ## GREEN LIGHT

If you understand that this question offers you an opportunity to accentuate your own experiences, accomplishments, and qualities. There are bad bosses out there, but a savvy candidate should be able to put a supervisor's failures in a positive context. If you say your boss was "stingy with his knowledge," you are accentuating your desire to learn. In the same vein, saying that a manager was "uninvolved" could indicate your desire to work within a cohesive team. Just prepare—and practice—your responses ahead of time.

RED LIGHT

Any negativity.

Any attempt to blame the boss for your failures:

> *"You know, I had to really work hard to learn how to sell spice racks in the South Pacific, but it sure didn't help that my boss had never sold a darn thing to anyone. She seemed to think that everything I did was wrong and constantly called me out of the field for 'evaluations.' I spent so much time filling out unnecessary reports for her and attending meetings to discuss why I wasn't reaching my unrealistic quota that I never had a chance to succeed. I hope my new boss just leaves me alone."*

 LOOKING BACK NOW, IS THERE ANYTHING YOU COULD HAVE DONE TO IMPROVE YOUR RELATIONSHIP WITH THAT SUPERVISOR?

 GREEN LIGHT

Of course there is (presuming you are smart enough to grasp the lifesaver the interviewer just flung overboard). The work experience you've had since has shown you how to better accept criticism. Now that you have a better understanding of the pressures your supervisors are under, you can more successfully anticipate their needs. Use this opportunity to demonstrate your experience, perceptiveness, and maturity.

 RED LIGHT

> *"Nah, not with that dumb so-and-so. He reveled in our misery. I'm glad we put sugar in his gas tank!"*

WHAT WERE THE MOST MEMORABLE ACCOMPLISHMENTS AT YOUR LAST JOB? IN YOUR CAREER?

 ## WHAT DO THEY WANT TO HEAR?

Focus on your most recent accomplishments, those in your current position or the job you had just prior to this one. But make sure they are relevant to the position for which you're interviewing.

For example, a friend of mine who had been an editor for years answered this question by talking at length about the times she'd been asked to write promotional copy for the marketing department. She was trying to change careers so she deliberately tried to shift the interviewer's attention from her editing experience to her accomplishments as a marketing copywriter.

It's also wise to think about why you were able to achieve these peaks in your career. For example,

> *"I really stopped to listen to what my customers wanted, rather than just trying to sell them."*

> *"I realized I needed to know a lot more about Subchapter-S corporations, so I enrolled in a tax seminar."*

This type of response tells the interviewer you give a great deal of thought to how you will reach your goals rather than blindly plunging ahead in their general direction. By letting the interviewer know that you are in the practice of regularly assessing your shortcomings, you'll show that you are better able to find the means to overcome them.

 ## RED LIGHT

Bragging about accomplishments that have nothing to do with the requirements for this job.

Citing (proudly or otherwise) frivolous, meaningless, minor, or dubious accomplishments:

> *"I finally managed to get out of bed every morning and get to work on time."*

> *"I personally raised $25 for the volunteer fire department."*

> *"I successfully typed all my boss's correspondence the same week it was handed to me, even if I had to work all day."*

 WHAT IS THE BIGGEST FAILURE YOU'VE HAD IN YOUR CAREER? WHAT STEPS HAVE YOU TAKEN TO MAKE SURE SOMETHING LIKE THAT DOESN'T HAPPEN AGAIN?

 WHAT DO THEY WANT TO HEAR?

Before you start spilling your guts, remember that the interviewer is not a priest and you are not in a confessional! In this situation, it would be foolhardy to produce a detailed log of your every shortcoming, misstep, and misdeed. But it would be equally silly to pretend you're perfect and have never experienced failure in the course of your career, education, or life.

The best approach is to admit to one weakness or failure—make it a good one!—and then talk about the steps you are taking (or have taken) to make sure that you'll never fail in quite that way again.

What makes a failure not so bad or a weakness seem acceptable? Good question! Choose any deficiency that might be considered a plus in a slightly different light. For example:

- ● You have a tendency to take on too much yourself. You're trying to solve this problem by delegating more.

- You're impatient with delays. So you're trying to better understand every step of the process a product must go through in order to anticipate holdups in the future.

- You've realized you're a workaholic. But you're doing your best to remedy your condition by reading books on time management.

Try to think of a failure that took place relatively early in your career and/or one that would seem completely unrelated to the work you would be performing for your new employer.

Don't ever admit to any personal quality that might hamper job performance, such as procrastination, laziness, or lack of concentration.

 GREEN LIGHT

Acknowledge a failure for which you do not appear to be fully responsible. (When I'm interviewing someone, the way a successful candidate scores the most points is to make it obvious she wasn't fully responsible for an admitted failure but is ready, nevertheless, to shoulder all the blame.)

If you must cite a job-related failure, be prepared to convince the interviewer that you now recognize what your error was and offer concrete examples that illustrate the lessons you learned.

 RED LIGHT

Claiming that you've never failed.

Citing a non-work related failure.

Your inability to offer any evidence that you are prepared to take responsibility for whatever failure is cited nor any proof that any changes were made as a result.

Don't declare, "It can never happen again." This is an unrealistic assessment that will call your judgment into question.

Never confess a huge work-related weakness: "I've always hated my bosses, every one. But I think I'll like you!"

VARIATIONS

- *What's your greatest weakness?*

- *What's the worst decision you ever made?*

- *What would you say is the biggest problem you've so far failed to overcome?*

A good interviewer will, based on the answers to questions like those above, continue to probe and put you on the spot, searching for details, details, and more details. If, for example, you say your greatest weakness is a fear of delegating because it always seems you can get it done faster/better yourself, you might be asked, "Tell me about the last time you should have delegated but didn't. What happened? Would you do it that way again? Would you do it differently today?"

Such probing can also help the interviewer assess your character: how you react to stress; how well you handle pressure, failure, or success; your own standards of success and failure; and how willing you are to assume responsibility, especially for decisions or outcomes that weren't your fault.

 ## HAVE YOU MANAGED PEOPLE IN ANY OF THE POSITIONS YOU'VE HELD?

 ## WHAT DO THEY WANT TO HEAR?

Moving up in most companies (and in most careers) means managing people. If you are interviewing for a supervisory position or for a job that typically leads to a management track, the interviewer will try to probe your potential in this area.

So it's best to answer this question positively, *even if you have never actually managed anyone on the job.* Candidates with experience managing other people are considered more mature, whether or not their subordinates considered them good leaders. What's important is that they earned the confidence of their employers.

If this is you, be sure to give the interviewer specific details on how many people you supervised and in what capacities these people worked.

What if you haven't actually had people reporting to you? You may want to substitute the word "leadership" for "management" and talk about the clubs and other activities in which you managed members or volunteers or built consensus within the group. If these experiences have convinced you that you have the right stuff to be a good manager, by all means say so.

 ## GREEN LIGHT

Not just management experience, but managing the same (or a slightly higher) number of people in a similarly sized and similarly directed department or division.

A positive appreciation of the varying skills needed to manage and motivate different types of employees, especially if you never actually managed anyone on the job.

 ## RED LIGHT

No management experience for a job that requires you manage people. (Remember, red light means an answer that may make the interviewer stop and think, not necessarily one that will automatically eliminate you. If companies only hired people who have managed others, how would they ever grow their own stars?)

Any negative expression of management experience. ("Yes, I managed two people at my last firm and let me tell you, they were both overpaid do-nothings!")

Don't give the impression that you underestimate the requirements of management, thinking it's just a move up in position and money but not appreciating the pressures of increased responsibility, new skills needed, and so on. And don't appear unwilling to work to acquire them.

 TELL ME ABOUT THE TYPES OF PEOPLE YOU HAVE TROUBLE GETTING ALONG WITH.

 WHAT DO THEY WANT TO HEAR?

This could be a land mine for a candidate who responds too quickly, saying "pushy, abrasive people" only to find out later that the interviewer is known for being brusque.

 GREEN LIGHT

One person I interviewed gave me what I thought was a good answer to this question:

> *"I was discussing this problem with my boss just the other day. He told me I'm too impatient with slow performers. That the world is filled with 'C,' rather than 'A' or 'B' people, and I expect them all to be great performers. So, I guess I do have trouble with mediocre and poor workers. I don't expect to ever accept poor work, but I'm learning to be more patient."*

Was he *really* discussing this "just the other day?" Did the conversation ever take place? Probably not, but who cares? It's a nice touch! And the answer works, too. Shouldn't any top candidate be impatient with slow performers? He even discussed what he's doing to solve his "problem." Short and sweet—and very much to the point.

RED LIGHT

A general, vague answer indicates both a lack of analysis and a dearth of self-knowledge. Of course, you don't really want to answer this question, which is why it was asked. But you certainly should know that it and its brethren—"What's your greatest weakness?" "Tell me about your worst boss." "Tell me about your greatest failure."—are potentially on the agenda.

VARIATION

- *What types of people have trouble getting along with you?*

 WHAT DO THEY WANT TO HEAR?

If you say "none," the interviewer will assume you're being evasive, stupid, or both. So be ready with an answer. I suggest thinking of an anecdote, a short story that softens with humor the reasons someone disliked you.

A friend of mine remembered back to his first job. Just out of college, he was the first new hire in his department within a state agency in six years. Eager to succeed, he hit the ground running. From day one, he worked twice as fast as his long-term peers, who, needless to say, resented him for it. So his answer was ready-made—and pretty much unverifiable—making it a perfect dodge.

 WHO DO YOU THINK ARE OUR TWO (OR THREE OR FIVE) MAJOR COMPETITORS?

 WHAT DO THEY WANT TO HEAR?

It doesn't belong in this group of questions, but some interviewers like asking this question (or something like it) as early in the process as possible. It will quickly and painfully reveal the depth or shallowness of your preinterview research. If you clearly have a handle on the company's place in the industry and can adequately, even intelligently, discuss its products, its strengths and weaknesses versus the competition, the health of the industry, and so on, you are a *serious* candidate. Granted, it says absolutely nothing about your particular qualifications for the job, but if you *are* qualified, this display of knowledge may well be that little extra that separates you from other qualified (or even slightly *more* qualified) candidates.

Although a lot of hemming, hawing, and nail-biting—along with an obvious lack of an answer—may not automatically lead to your dismissal, I would personally consider it a black mark.

VARIATIONS

- *What's our greatest advantage over our competitors?*

- *What's our biggest disadvantage?*

- *Which of our new products do you think has the greatest potential for growth?*

- *What do you think is the greatest challenge facing our company? Our industry?*

NOW *REALLY* TELL ME ABOUT YOURSELF

In the world of business, style has little to do with how well you dress (although at some companies, and in some positions, the "right" wardrobe may be a defining element of the culture). Typically, your business style is a measure—and often a subjective measure, at that—of how you conduct or will conduct yourself on the job.

How well do you get along with superiors? Subordinates? Peers? What's your management philosophy? Do you like to work alone or be part of a team? Interviewers will ask these types of questions to assess how you'll act and interact on the job.

And interviewers will undoubtedly base at least some of their hiring decisions on their feelings about each candidate's attitude. In every case, they are assessing how the candidate's style fits in with the organizational culture, their own style, and/or the team's style. So, in general, a "green light" is any answer that will convince the interviewer he or she has found a positive fit, and a "red light" is an answer that reveals differences of style substantive enough to give an interviewer pause. Rather than characterizing an answer as inherently right or wrong, in other words, most interviewers are simply trying to ascertain whether you will get along with Joe or Sally or Jimmy—the other members of the company, department, or team.

Following is a series of "style" questions you should probably expect to be asked somewhere along the way.

 ARE YOU AN ORGANIZED PERSON?

 WHAT DO THEY WANT TO HEAR?

Even if you firmly believe that a neat desk is the sign of a sick mind, talk in detail about the organizational skills that you have developed—time management, project management, needs assessment, delegation—and how those skills have made you more effective.

But don't veer too closely to either extreme. No one wants to hire someone so anal-retentive that he always knows the number of paper clips in his drawer or someone so *dis*organized that she'd be lucky if she remembers it's Monday.

VARIATIONS

- *Paint me a mental picture of your current office.*
- *Describe the top of your desk.*

- *Tell me about the first five files in your file cabinet.*
- *Tell me about the first 60 minutes of a typical day.*

 DO YOU MANAGE YOUR TIME WELL?

 WHAT DO THEY WANT TO HEAR?

I hope you can truthfully say yes, that you are a self-starter and almost never procrastinate. And if you *can't* say it truthfully, I hope you're smart enough to realize now is not the time to wail about your broken alarm clock—which is why, by the way, you were 15 minutes late for the interview, as you now remind the interviewer. Good employees are able to set goals; prioritize their tasks; and devote adequate, and appropriate, amounts of time to each one.

In answering a rather conceptual question like this one (and what could be more conceptual than time?), try to sprinkle in specifics. Here are a few examples:

> *"I rarely miss a deadline. When circumstances beyond my control interfere, I make up the time lost as quickly as possible."*

> *"I establish a To-Do list first thing in the morning. Then I add to it, and reprioritize tasks, if necessary, as the day goes on."*

> *"I really like interacting with the people I work with. But when I need to focus on detailed tasks, I make sure to set aside time that will be free of interruptions of any kind, so I can concentrate and work more effectively."*

 HOW DO YOU HANDLE CHANGE?

 WHAT DO THEY WANT TO HEAR?

I hope that you are able to say that you handle change well. Business is about change. In order to remain competitive, companies have to adapt to changes in technology, personnel, leadership, business structure, the types of services they deliver, and even the products they produce. And their people need to change just as quickly.

Choose an example of a change you've faced that's resulted in something positive. Try to show that you not only accepted change and adapted to it, but flourished because of it:

> *"Recently, my boss decided our company needed to develop a virtual storefront on the Web. I was given the task, along with a designer, of taking the project from the research phase to operation in eight weeks. I didn't have any special expertise in the area of computers and online communications, so I have to assume I was given the task because I adapt well.*
>
> *"We researched the subject, examined the alternatives, and presented a plan that was accepted. Then I worked with the designer to present information in a medium neither of us had ever worked with before. In our second month online, sales were up 7 percent over the same time last year."*

 HOW DO YOU GO ABOUT MAKING IMPORTANT DECISIONS?

 WHAT DO THEY WANT TO HEAR?

By now, you have some sense of the culture of the company you're interested in working for. So shade your answer to match it.

For example, if you want to work for a financial services company, you probably don't want to portray yourself as a manager who makes decisions based on gut feelings rather than hard data. Similarly, if you're auditioning to be an air traffic controller, it's best not to admit that you like to sleep on things before making up your mind.

Think in terms of the interviewer's main concerns: Will you need to be analytical? Creative? Willing to call on the expertise of others?

If you are bucking for a management position, you'll also want to take this opportunity to convince the interviewer that your relationship skills have made you management material . . . or at least set you on the way to achieving that goal.

You might say something like this:

> *"When I'm faced with an important decision,*
> *I ask the advice of others. I try to consider every-*
> *thing. But ultimately, I'm the one who decides.*
> *I guess that's why they say, 'It's lonely at the top.'*
> *The higher you go in management, the more*
> *responsibility you have and the more decisions*
> *you have to make by yourself."*

Although this is a nice general answer, you may run into an interviewer who decides to probe to see if the "rubber meets the road," following up with something like, "Okay, tell me about the last important decision you had to make, how you went about making it, and the results you achieved." Can you match in particulars the nice general answer given above? Or do you inadvertently show you do things completely differently (better or worse) than you just said you did?

 ## DO YOU WORK WELL UNDER PRESSURE?

 ## WHAT DO THEY WANT TO HEAR?

Naturally, everyone will say yes to this question. However, it will be best to provide examples that support your claim to being the Second Coming of Cool Hand Luke. Be sure to choose anecdotes that don't imply that the pressure you've faced has resulted from your own procrastination or failure to anticipate problems.

VARIATIONS

● *Tell me about the last time pressure led you to inde- cision, a poor decision, or a mistake. What would you have done differently? Have you found yourself in a similar situation since? What did you do?*

The questioning pattern I am suggesting you prepare for throughout this book should be apparent by now: Good inter- viewers will probe, probe, then probe some more. Why? Because they figure you can only rehearse so many generaliza- tions and remember a limited number of little white lies, so the more detailed their questions, the more likely you will inadvertently reveal any misrepresentations, exaggerations, or omissions.

 DO YOU ANTICIPATE PROBLEMS WELL OR MERELY REACT TO THEM?

 WHAT DO THEY WANT TO HEAR?

All managers panic from time to time. The best learn to protect themselves by anticipating problems that might lie around the bend. For example, one sales manager I know had his staff provide reports on all positive—and negative—budget variances on a weekly basis. By sharing this valuable information with his boss and also with the manufacturing, distribution, and market- ing arms of the company, he helped improve product turnover and boost flagging sales. This kind of story is terrific fodder for successful interviews, and it's the kind of example you should be trying to provide.

ARE YOU A RISK TAKER OR DO YOU PREFER
TO PLAY IT SAFE?

 WHAT DO THEY WANT TO HEAR?

In most cases, the ideal candidate will be a little of both. Inter-viewers who ask this question are probing for intimations of in-novation and creativity. Are you the shepherd or just one of the flock? But they also want to find out whether you might turn into a loose cannon who will ignore company policies and be all too ready to lead a fatal cavalry charge.

Again, this is a highly (company) cultural question. The in-terviewer might personally prefer Stonewall Jackson, CEO, to be leading his troops into battle but probably wouldn't want him to be Controller.

VARIATIONS

- *Tell me about the last time you took a risk. Was it the right decision? What would you have done differently?*

 IF YOU COULD START YOUR CAREER OVER
AGAIN, WHAT WOULD YOU DO DIFFERENTLY?

 WHAT DO THEY WANT TO HEAR?

Interviewers use hypothetical questions to get candidates to think on their feet. They expect you to "know your lines" when it comes to the facts about your career and education. But how will you react when you have to drop your guard and ad lib?

Unless you're shooting for a complete change of career, you must convince the interviewer that you wouldn't change a thing. You love your career and, given the chance, you'd do it all over again.

Feel free to quote Paul Anka (via Sinatra): "Regrets? I've had a few. But all in all, too few to mention." In this case, however, watch which ones you *do* mention, and make sure you position them in a way that shows what you've learned. Did you leave your first job because you were too impatient for a promotion, only to realize you hadn't learned all you could have? Did you miss the opportunity to specialize in some area or develop a particular expertise that you should have?

 GREEN LIGHT

> *"My only regret is that I didn't go in this direction sooner. I started my career in editorial, and I enjoyed that. But once I got into marketing, I found I really loved it. Now, I can't wait to get to work every day."*

 RED LIGHT

> *"I wish I had never gotten into magazine publishing in the first place. But now I guess I'm stuck. And to think, I could have been editing garden books for FernMoor Press. . . ."*

VARIATION

● *What was the biggest mistake you ever made when choosing a job?*

 DO YOU PREFER TO WORK BY YOURSELF OR WITH OTHERS?

 WHAT DO THEY WANT TO HEAR?

Again, the position you're interviewing for will dictate how you should shape your answer. For example, if you're interviewing for a job as an on-the-road sales rep (who may develop an unhealthy crush on his rental car but will otherwise interact solely with customers, waitresses, and hotel employees), you *won't* want to admit that you thrive on your relationships with coworkers and can't *imagine* working without a lot of interaction.

Even if you do like the interaction at work, don't try to paint your environment as a bed of roses without any thorns. You know the old saying, "You can choose your friends, but you can't choose your relatives." That goes for coworkers, too.

Every job situation forces us to get along with people we might not choose to socialize with. But we must get along with them and, quite often, for long stretches of time and under difficult circumstances. Acknowledging this shows strength. Talk about how you've managed to get along with a variety of other people.

 ## GREEN LIGHT

Once I was interviewing candidates for a position managing a production department with 16 employees. Production departments in publishing companies are filled with some of the quirkiest people you'll ever come across, so I had to gauge the interpersonal skills of each applicant very carefully.

After I'd asked one candidate a couple of questions about his management and communication skills, he gave me a steady look and said,

> *"Look, you know and I know it's not always easy*
> *to manage artists and proofreaders. I do my best to*
> *convince them of the importance of deadlines and*
> *let them know what it costs us when we miss them.*
> *I also point out how unfair it is to others in the*

*department, and to the entire operation, when
things are held up unnecessarily.*

*"I usually find some way to get along with all of
the people in the department, some way to convince
them that timeliness and accuracy are absolute
musts. It's not always easy. But a lot of times it's
fun. When we are rushed because another department is late, I use this as an object lesson. The most
important thing is to distribute the work fairly and
let everyone know that you expect them to do their
share."*

Needless to say, this right-on answer won the job.

VARIATIONS

- *How do you get along with your superior(s)? With
  your coworkers? With your subordinates?*

- *How much time per week do you spend working
  alone? Do you think it should be more? Less?*

- *Do you enjoy doing individual research?*

 WHAT DO THEY WANT TO HEAR?

The answers to these questions should, first of all, bear some
relation to the answers to earlier questions about people with
whom you have had trouble or those who have had trouble getting along with you. (Consistency, consistency, consistency!) But
this is, again, a highly cultural question, and one in which the
requirements of the job define the "rightness" of any answer. If
you thrive on working alone but the interviewer is seeking
someone who will always be part of a team, the dichotomy will
be obvious.

HOW DO YOU GENERALLY HANDLE CONFLICT?

 WHAT DO THEY WANT TO HEAR?

> *"I really don't get angry with other people very often. I'm usually able to work things out or anticipate problems before they occur. When conflicts can't be avoided, I don't back down. But I certainly do try to be reasonable."*

Or,

> *"I've had confrontations with coworkers who weren't holding up their end of a job. I feel that employees owe it to their bosses, customers, and coworkers to do their jobs properly."*

 HOW DO YOU BEHAVE WHEN YOU HAVE A PROBLEM WITH A COWORKER?

 WHAT DO THEY WANT TO HEAR?

> *"I had to work with a designer who was obstinate about listening to any of my suggestions. He would answer me in monosyllables and then drag his feet before doing anything I requested. Finally, I said, 'Look, we're both professionals. Neither of us has the right answer all the time. I have noticed that you don't really like my suggestions. But rather than resist implementing them, why don't we just discuss what you don't like?'*

> *"That worked like a charm. In fact, we eventually became friends."*

VARIATIONS

- *Tell me about the last time you lost your temper.*

- *Tell me about the last time you disagreed with your boss. A coworker. A subordinate. What did you do and what was the result?*

 ## HOW DO YOU MOTIVATE PEOPLE?

 ## WHAT DO THEY WANT TO HEAR?

A good answer will note how it "depends on the person," then offer one or two concrete examples. A poor candidate will imply that all people are motivated by the same thing or can be motivated with the same approach, a kind of one-size-fits-all philosophy. A savvy interviewer will use this as a follow-up question to "What is your management philosophy?"

 # SOMETIMES YOU JUST CAN'T WIN

Some people have always had a job—in fact, a lot of jobs. And companies are especially cautious about hiring people who have changed jobs repeatedly. Curiously enough, however, many are equally cautious about hiring people who have never moved. If either of these situations describes your particular job history, here's how to handle it.

 ## YOU'VE CHANGED JOBS QUITE FREQUENTLY. HOW DO WE KNOW YOU'LL STICK AROUND?

 ## WHAT DO THEY WANT TO HEAR?

The hiring process is expensive for companies and time-consuming for managers. Job-hoppers only serve to make it a more frequent process. So, in framing your reply, convince the interviewer you have staying power by painting the position on offer as your career's "promised land."

 GREEN LIGHT

Take one of the following two approaches:

- Confess that you had some difficulty defining your career goals at first, but now you are quite sure of your direction.

- Convince the interviewer that you left previous positions only after you realized that moving on was the only way to increase your responsibilities and broaden your experience.

Be sure to emphasize the fact that you would like nothing better than to stay and grow with a company. Here's an example to study if you have to explain your own job-hopping history.

Sherri had four jobs in the first six years after college graduation. Her clever reply to an interviewer's skepticism about her staying power combines both techniques:

"All through college, I was convinced that I wanted to be a programmer. But after a few months in my first job, I found that I was unhappy. Naturally, I blamed the company and the job. So when an opportunity opened up at Lakeside Bank, I grabbed it. But not long after the initial euphoria wore off, I was unhappy again.

"By this time I'd noticed that I really did enjoy the part of my job that dealt with applications. So when I heard about the job in end-user computing at SafeInvest, I went for it. I learned a lot there,

until I hit a 'glass ceiling.' It was a small firm, so there was no place for me to grow.

"I was recruited for the applications position at Deep Pockets Bank, and I got the job because of some of the innovations I'd developed at SI. The work has been terrific. But once again, I find that I'm a one-person department.

"This position offers the opportunity to manage a department and interact with programmers and applications specialists on the cutting edge of technology. Throughout my career, the one thing that has remained constant is my love of learning. This job would give me the chance to learn so much."

 YOU'VE BEEN WITH THE SAME ORGANIZATION FOR ___ YEARS. WON'T YOU HAVE A TOUGH TIME GETTING USED TO A NEW CULTURE, COMPANY, ATMOSPHERE, TEAM?

 WHAT DO THEY WANT TO HEAR?

The flip side of the previous question. Here's what the interviewer is doing to you: If you've moved around, she questions your staying power. If you stuck with a single company, she questions your initiative. Lose-lose.

Here's how to fight back: During your tenure with your current company, you've probably worked for more than one boss. You may even have supervised many different types of people in various departments. Certainly you've teamed up with a variety of coworkers. And from inside this one organization, you've had a chance to observe a wide variety of other organizations—competitors, vendors, customers, and so on. Get it?

You're flexible—and loyal. You should remind the interviewer that this can prove to be a valuable combination.

VARIATION

● *You've been with your current employer for only a short amount of time. Is this an indication that you'll be moving around a lot throughout your career?*

By the time you've been asked introductory questions, questions about high school and college experiences, and these preliminary on-the-job questions, you should certainly have an idea of whether you are still a viable candidate. And if you are, you can expect even more questions. (If you are not, you may politely be led to the door any time now.)

If the interviewer is still unsure, it's time for her to ask even more detailed questions. She's invited you to paint her a picture. Okay, Rembrandt, what else do you have to offer her?

TIPS FOR HANDLING QUESTIONS ABOUT WORK

- **BE HONEST.** But play up your strengths and whitewash your weaknesses. If you have to talk about negative experiences, point out what you learned from them and why you wouldn't make the same mistakes again.

- **INTRODUCE ONLY POSITIVES.** Don't give away information that could come back to haunt you.

- **STRIKE A BALANCE BETWEEN PORTRAYING YOURSELF AS A COMPANY MAN OR WOMAN AND A LOOSE CANNON.** Screening interviewers and hiring managers are often attracted to risk takers. But they also put a lot of stock in playing by the rules. Your preinterview research should clarify which road to take. If in doubt, choose neither; settle for a balanced reply.

- **USE SPECIFIC WORK SITUATIONS TO SUBSTANTIATE YOUR CLAIMS.** If you sense the interview drifting into subjectivity, regain the upper hand by citing concrete examples from your past experience. Don't just *say* you're organized. Tell *how* you organized a complex project from beginning to end. Remember, insofar as possible, you want the interviewer basing his or her decision on the *facts*—your strengths, qualifications, and accomplishments—not some subjective evaluation of "chemistry."

- **CHOOSE YOUR WORDS CAREFULLY.** Make sure that you are indeed answering questions and not suggesting other areas the interviewer hadn't thought to explore. For example, I suggest, "I'm looking for greater challenges," rather than, "The boss didn't give me enough to do." Do you really want to travel down *that* road?

CHAPTER

Let's Focus on Some Specifics

N ow that the generalities have been covered—pesky things such as motivation and your basic on-the-job attitude—good interviewers will try to glean even more particular information about your past performance. Take heart; if you've made it this far, you're still a viable candidate!

 TELL ME ABOUT THE LAST TIME YOU . . .

- Made a mistake.

- Made a good decision.

- Made a poor decision.

- Fired someone.

- Hired someone.

- Were fired or laid off.

- Were asked to resign.

- Were denied a promotion.

- Learned a new skill.

- Developed a new expertise.

- Failed to complete a project on time.

- Found a unique solution to a problem.

- Found a creative solution to a problem.

- Found a cost-effective solution to a problem.

- Aimed too high.

- Aimed too low.

- Made (or lost) a great sale.

- Saved the company money.

- Went over budget.

- Exceeded your own expectations.

- Exceeded your boss's expectations.

- Fell short of your boss's expectations.

- Had to think on your feet.

- Had to make an unpopular decision.

- Had to implement an unpopular decision.

- Dealt with a difficult boss.

- Dealt with a difficult customer.

- Dealt with a difficult coworker.

- Dealt with a difficult subordinate.

- Were frustrated at work.

WHAT DO THEY WANT TO HEAR?

These are open-ended questions like "Tell me about yourself," encouraging you to talk but clearly requiring focused, specific answers. Follow-up questions should be obvious based on your initial answer: "Okay, I understand how the lack of divisional coordination led to the budget shortfall. And you have clearly taken responsibility for your part in the miscommunication. But what did you do to change procedures to ensure it didn't happen again? And, by the way, *did* it happen again?"

Expect a seasoned interviewer to keep probing and asking for more specifics, more examples, who said what, who did what, what were the results, what would you do differently now, what do you need to change to do better in the future, what *have* you changed, and so on.

GREEN LIGHT

A *specific* answer to a *specific* question, the more detailed the better.

An answer to any of the above questions that has a beginning, middle, and end, much like a good story: Here's what happened, here's what you did, here's what you learned.

Some of the questions *require* job-related answers; others may allow for examples chosen from outside activities, perhaps volunteer work, or any part of one's personal life. A savvy candidate will "mix and match" stories and examples to convince an interviewer she is well-rounded and actually has a life after 5 p.m.

Take appropriate credit for an accomplishment (reducing costs, increasing revenues, a creative solution, a tough sale), but be fair and honest enough to put your own contribution within the context of what your team/organization/boss/assistants did . . . and try to appear to be bending over backwards to do so.

Most interviewers will favor a candidate who has been around long enough to make good *and* bad decisions, good *and* bad hires, good and bad *choices.* The breadth of your exposure to the basic tenets of business is more important (to *me,* anyway) than the extent of your experience.

 RED LIGHT

Avoid giving the impression you're a "hard-working, self-starting, high-energy" Mr. Generalization who can't furnish an interviewer with too many examples of your wonderfulness, no matter how many softball questions she tosses you.

Most interviewers will be suspicious of someone with years of experience in the same job who seems to have enjoyed little exposure to the normal day-to-day vagaries of the world. You hired someone once and they were fine. Never fired anyone. Can't remember the last time you actually had to make a major decision.

No matter how talented you are (or think you are), avoid claiming to have been CEO/COO/CFO/Creative Star/Sales Guru—all at the same time. Even if you are a prodigy who would give Mozart pause, you should be savvy enough not to take credit for every success your company achieved in the last decade (especially if you've only been there three years!).

I always found it interesting, for example, that seven different independent publicists approached me at a trade show and that every single one of them claimed—in their literature and even on their business cards—to be totally responsible for the success of the book *Chicken Soup for the Soul.* While I'm not sure every one of them had even *worked* on the book, clearly not every one of them was singularly in charge of the publicity plan!

 WHAT DO YOU DO WHEN YOU'RE HAVING TROUBLE . . .

- **Solving a problem?**
- **With a subordinate?**

- **With a boss?**

- **With your job?**

 WHAT DO YOU DO WHEN . . .

- **Things are slow?**

- **Things are hectic?**

- **You're burned out?**

- **You have multiple priorities (family/ work/school/etc.)?**

 WHAT DO THEY WANT TO HEAR?

These questions are just further attempts to figure out how you think and act. You may well have been asked—10 or 30 minutes ago—about problems with a boss, coworkers, and the like, so be careful. A good interviewer may be trying to trip you up by honing in on the same issue from a different direction. The style of question framed along the lines of "What do you do when . . ." is very different from "Do you have a problem with . . . ?"

 WHAT SKILLS DO YOU MOST NEED TO ACQUIRE/DEVELOP TO ADVANCE YOUR CAREER?

 WHAT DO THEY WANT TO HEAR?

You should claim to be developing a skill in line with the job for which you're interviewing, otherwise why are you talking about it? "Well, I really need to grip my tennis racquet more firmly at the net. My stroke is just all wrong." *Oookay.*

Let me rephrase that:

 WHAT DO YOUR SUPERVISORS TEND TO CRITICIZE
MOST ABOUT YOUR PERFORMANCE?

 WHAT DO THEY WANT TO HEAR?

This is another way of framing a series of questions you've probably already been asked: What's your greatest weakness? What was your greatest failure? What would your supervisor say about you?

Asking what amounts to the same question three or four different ways can help a seasoned interviewer ferret out the inconsistencies you might well reveal.

 GREEN LIGHT

You should certainly assume your references will be checked and your current supervisor contacted, so your answer better match what your supervisor says.

Consider discussing an evaluation from an earlier job, switching to what you did about it, and claiming that your current supervisor would, therefore, not consider it a problem any longer.

Just remember that a good interviewer will find a way to get around this elegant subterfuge: "Was there anything your current supervisor criticized you for in your last performance evaluation?" or "What specific areas did your current supervisor's last evaluation indicate you needed to work on?"

 RED LIGHT

Never cite a personal quality that might (or convince the interviewer that it might) hamper your job performance, such as procrastination, laziness, lack of concentration, a hot temper, or tardiness.

Most interviewers probably will be suspicious if you claim never to have received a poor evaluation. While not necessarily untrue—there are companies and bosses that fail to do systematic evaluations or fail to take them very seriously—it will probably just lead you to this follow-up question: "Tell me about the last time your boss criticized you. What was it for? What was your response? What have you done to fix/solve/change what he criticized?" I *would* find it highly suspect for any candidate to claim they have *never* been called on the carpet for *any*thing.

 ## DID YOU INAUGURATE NEW PROCEDURES (SYSTEMS, POLICIES, ETC.) IN YOUR PREVIOUS POSITION? TELL ME ABOUT THEM.

 ## WHAT DO THEY WANT TO HEAR?

Of course! You had some very good solutions you'd be happy to share with the interviewer. Regrettably, however, some (or none?) could be implemented because of circumstances beyond your control.

You don't have to be a divisional president or department head to answer this question. An administrative assistant may have creatively instituted a new filing system or a better way to delegate departmental correspondence, or simply utilized technology to improve a mundane task, like keeping the boss's calendar.

The interviewer is seeking industriousness, creativity, and concern for the organization and its success. So this is the time to bring up those facts and figures we talked about earlier. Describe the changes or improvements you were responsible for making and identify how they helped the company increase profits, save money, or improve production (or all three!).

VARIATION

● *Was there anything your company (or department or team) could have done to be more successful?*

Here's a perfectly acceptable answer:

"Sure, we could have expanded our product line, perhaps even doubled it, to take advantage of our superior distribution. But we just didn't have the capital and couldn't get the financing."

 HAVE YOU BEEN IN CHARGE OF BUDGETING, APPROVING EXPENSES, AND MONITORING DEPARTMENTAL PROGRESS AGAINST FINANCIAL GOALS? ARE YOU VERY QUALIFIED IN THIS AREA?

 WHAT DO THEY WANT TO HEAR?

Again, financial responsibility signals an employer's faith in you. If you haven't had many—or any—fiscal duties, admit it. But as always, nothing is stopping you from being creative in the way you frame your reply. Here's an example:

"Well, I've never actually run a department, but I've had to set and meet budgetary goals for several projects I've worked on. In fact, I did this so often that I took a class to learn how to set up and use Microsoft Excel spreadsheets."

If you've had broader responsibilities, talk about your approval authority. What is the largest expenditure you could sign off on? Let the interviewer know, in round numbers, the income and expenses of the departments you've supervised.

Be careful. This question is also designed to trap you if you lied to the previous question. "So you managed 14 people but had no financial responsibilities at all? *Hmmm.*"

If you answer this question *positively,* expect more probing: "In your experience, what were the most common obstacles you faced when completing assignments or projects on time and on budget? Give me one or two examples and tell me how you dealt with them."

 HAVE YOU EVER FIRED ANYONE? WHY?

 WHAT DO THEY WANT TO HEAR?

Even if you had good reason, you know that firing someone is never pleasant. Say so, and provide a "sanitized" (and brief!) version of the events to the interviewer. Remember, you don't want to seem like a negative person, one who might disrupt an entire department. But you don't want to appear *too* empathetic.

You should express a modicum of sympathy for the person (people) who got the ax (you clearly didn't relish your role), an understanding that sometimes people have to be fired (business is business), and a readiness to do it appropriately, professionally, and compassionately when required.

 GREEN LIGHT

Let's say you fired someone for not meeting productivity goals. You might be thinking, "Boy, I'm glad I got rid of that bum. He was nothing but a wimp and whiner who never did a good day's work in all the time he was on the job." Go ahead and *think* that. But when you open your mouth, *say* something like this:

> *"Yes, I fired someone who continually fell short of his productivity goals. His shortcomings were documented and discussed with him over a period of months. But in that time he failed to show any real*

> *improvement. I had no choice. As a supervisor, I*
> *want everyone in my department to work out. Let's*
> *face it, though, not everyone is equally dedicated to*
> *his or her job."*

If you haven't actually fired anyone, here is one way to respond:

> *"I've never actually fired anyone myself, but it was*
> *the policy at my company that no hirings or firings*
> *should be unilateral. I was asked on two occasions to*
> *give my opinion about someone else's performance.*
> *It's never easy to be honest about a coworker's short-*
> *comings. But I felt I had to do what was best for the*
> *department and fair to everyone else in it."*

 HAVE YOU EVER HIRED ANYONE? WHY DID YOU CHOOSE THEM?

 WHAT DO THEY WANT TO HEAR?

If you have hired one or more people during your career, your answer might go something like this:

> *"Yes, I have hired people. I have also decided*
> *whether some internal applicants were right for*
> *jobs in my department. The first time I hired some-*
> *one, I concentrated on checking off all the right*
> *qualifications. I just went down a checklist.*
>
> *"Since then, though, I've learned that some candi-*
> *dates who became excellent workers didn't*
> *necessarily have every qualification on that*
> *checklist. They more than make up for what they*
> *lacked in the beginning with enthusiasm and a*
> *willingness to work with others."*

What if you've never hired anyone? Show the interviewer you appreciate that he or she is trying to evaluate both your management potential and people skills, and try something like this:

> *"Not really, but on several occasions I was asked to speak to prospective applicants and offer my opinion. Of course, in those cases, I was trying to determine whether that person would be a team player and if he or she would get along with the other people in the department."*

 ## LET'S TAKE IT FROM THE TOP

If you're seeking an executive-level position, most of the previous questions in this book are just as pertinent as if you were interviewing to be a receptionist (although the interviewer would expect a different level of answer!). Here are a few questions you can expect if you are a potential CFO, CIO, or Executive Vice President:

 ## WHAT'S THE MOST DIFFICULT PART OF BEING A MANAGER OR EXECUTIVE?

Tell me about the last situation in which you were directed to overhaul a problem unit/department/division/company. What were you confronted with, what did you do, and what kind of culture did you attempt to create?

How many people did you hire and fire?

What goals did you establish?

How long was your outlook, and what were the results?

WHAT DO THEY WANT TO HEAR?

Every question is designed to get a handle on your management philosophy and gauge your abilities to conceptualize on a general basis and implement on a specific one: to create loyalty, unity, and shared goals; to create and produce under pressure; to stay within budget and/or produce over budget; and so on. Needless to say, you should cite very specific examples that detail the problems you faced, the actions you took, and the results you achieved.

VARIATIONS

- *What kinds of decisions are difficult for you to make?*

- *How do you go about making a decision?*

- *How do you decide what tasks to delegate and to whom?*

 HOW DO YOU "STAY IN THE LOOP"?

 WHAT DO THEY WANT TO HEAR?

There are many ways to get the information an interviewer is seeking with this question. Here are some variations:

- *How many meetings do you schedule/attend per week/month?*

- *Are you a MBWA (Management by Walking Around) aficionado?*

- *Do you spend a lot of time in your subordinates' offices asking questions, or do you prefer to wait for them to come to you with problems?*

All of the above are much more specific than "Explain your management philosophy," a question an experienced interviewee can wiggle through with a couple of business-guru quotes. The more senior your current position—and the more executive the position for which you're applying—the more likely these types of questions will be asked. And the more important the answers to them will be.

 ## HOW DO YOU DEAL WITH SUBORDINATES WHO ARE BECOMING PART OF THE PROBLEM RATHER THAN PART OF THE SOLUTION?

 ## WHAT DO THEY WANT TO HEAR?

This has been asked previously in other forms. The interviewer is trying to separate the real leaders from the "managers with a title" and to ascertain whether your particular style will mesh with the organizational culture.

 ## SEE THAT PICTURE FRAME ON THE WALL? SELL IT TO ME.

Or the pen, the desk, the paperweight, whatever. I'm not sure I particularly like this question, although it isn't one that should surprise an entry-level sales candidate.

 ## WHAT DO THEY WANT TO HEAR?

One of the major characteristics of a truly good salesperson is his or her ability to ask questions and listen to the answers (kind of like a really good interviewer). So a good sales candidate will begin by asking a series of questions about the object and about the interviewer's particular needs.

An old friend of mine, a sales superstar, once told me that if he asked enough questions, especially enough of the *right* questions, sooner or later every prospect would tell him exactly what he needed to say to get the sale.

Obviously, the ultimate test of a sales candidate is whether he or she is really capable of selling that object to the interviewer. What about the candidates who will have nothing to do with sales? Some interviewers may still consider this a viable question if only to see how they react under pressure. The less sales-oriented you are, the more this question may bother you.

MORE TIPS FOR ANSWERING QUESTIONS ABOUT WORK

- **BE POSITIVE** about your reasons for leaving your current job (or any previous jobs, for that matter). The key word to remember is "more." You want *more* responsibility, *more* challenges, *more* opportunity, and finally (but don't play this up, except as a natural consequence of the previous "mores"), *more* money.

- If you've been fired, **stress what you learned** from the experience. Be as positive as you can.

- **QUANTIFY** the confidence other employers have placed in you. Do this by stressing specific facts, figures, and measurable accomplishments. Mention the number of employees you've supervised, the amount of money you've controlled, and/or the earnings that your department achieved under your management.

- **NEVER SPEAK BADLY** of past supervisors or employers.

- Make the job you're interviewing for your chief objective. **Frame your answers** so that you let the interviewer know that you see this job as a means to achieving your ultimate career objectives. Be careful not to make it sound like either a stepping stone or a safe haven.

What Have You Been Doing?

Whether you have been working for 20 years or 20 days, it is human nature to focus on the most recent job, even if it boasted the shortest tenure, and even if a previous job was for years and the current one just for months. Why? Because the interviewer wants to know what you can do for him or her—right now—and the most current job offers the best available proof.

 WHY ARE YOU THINKING OF LEAVING YOUR CURRENT JOB?

 WHAT DO THEY WANT TO HEAR?

Obviously, no one wants to leave a job with which they are completely content (although some people routinely interview to keep in practice or explore other opportunities in their area or industry). But the last thing you want to do is appear negative or, worse, speak badly about your current employer. (Your interviewer will assume that if you're hired, you will soon be characterizing him and/or his company in the same disparaging terms.)

So handle your discontent (if that's what led you here) very gingerly. The less contented you are, the more careful you should be in talking about it. It will do you absolutely no good to confess to the interviewer that you lie awake nights fantasizing about putting a contract out on your current boss.

Instead, use what management consultants call "visioning": Imagine the ideal next step in your career, then act as though you are interviewing for that position.

Here's what I mean. Let's say you are interested in assuming more financial management responsibilities. You might tell the interviewer:

> *"There is a great deal I enjoy about my current job. But my potential for growth in this area is limited at Closely Held, Inc. because of the size of the company and the fact that expansion is not a part of its current strategic plan."*

GREEN LIGHT

Unless you've been fired or laid off, you should make it clear that you are sitting in front of the interviewer only because you seek more responsibility, a bigger challenge, and better opportunities for growth (even more money), *not* because you are desperate to put some distance between yourself and your current job situation.

Emphasize your desire to move *up* rather than just move *out*.

Avoid any personal and/or negative comments about coworkers, supervisors, or your current (last) company's policies.

RED LIGHT

Introducing any negative, no matter how horrible your current job situation. (In fact, the more obviously horrible your job, the more points you will score with many interviewers for creating an impression of relative contentment.)

A willingness to make a lateral move or even accept a demotion just to leave your current company. Unless you are moving into an entirely new area or field, such a willingness to move out rather than up would give *me* pause. What are you hiding? Is this just a last-ditch effort to get out before you are shoved out? And what does such an attitude say about your ability to tough it out until the right situation comes along? Is my company just a calmer sea in which to tread water until the right freighter passes by?

A candidate who admits she lies awake nights fantasizing about calling Joe "No Knees" Buzzano to "discipline" her current boss.

VARIATIONS

- *What's hindering your progress at your present firm?*

- *Is this the first time you've thought about leaving? What made you stay before?*

 WHERE DOES YOUR BOSS THINK YOU ARE NOW?

 WHAT DO THEY WANT TO HEAR?

Although you may have been given notice or laid off and, therefore, be interviewing with the full knowledge of your boss, it's more likely you're still employed. So under no circumstances mutter something like, "He thinks I'm interviewing with you so I can leave that hellhole behind. By the way, he'll be calling you tomorrow to find a job himself." You should attempt to schedule interviews during your lunch hour, after work, or on a personal or vacation day. I personally don't like to hear that a candidate has taken a sick day to talk with me. It's a white lie, but a lie nevertheless.

GREEN LIGHT

The truth, whatever it is. Many interviewers will give you points for demonstrating your sense of responsibility to your current job by scheduling a breakfast interview or one during a lunch hour or after work.

RED LIGHT

If you have blatantly lied or indicate through body language that the question makes you uncomfortable (implying that you lied).

If your answer demonstrates little or no loyalty to the company that's still paying the bills, whether that organization is enlightened or despotic.

ARE YOU STILL EMPLOYED AT THE LAST FIRM LISTED ON YOUR RESUME?

WHAT DO THEY WANT TO HEAR?

You probably know the adage that it's always easier to find a job when you already have one. Well, it's true, because many interviewers believe that an employed person is somehow better than an unemployed one, even if the latter is more qualified. Being laid off is perceived by many interviewers as a sign of weakness. I even heard one experienced executive recruiter say, "Oh, if she was laid off, there must be something wrong with her. Companies don't ever let really good employees go!" Would that it were true!

But the fact is that massive layoffs, while not as frequent or disruptive as a few years ago, can and do still occur. And many hard-working, loyal individuals who contributed greatly to their companies—and could be significant assets to a new one—have to admit they've been laid off. Personally, I am firmly convinced that there is no shame in this status and give a laid-off candidate the same consideration I do anyone else. I would not assume all interviewers are as enlightened.

What if you *were* fired? Come clean quickly and smoothly turn this potential negative into a positive.

Let's consider the case of Nick. A hotel sales manager, he was unfortunate enough to work for a petty tyrant who made a practice of taking Nick and his coworkers to task often, publicly and mercilessly.

One day, Nick finally had it. He blew up at his boss—and was fired on the spot. Later on, he was asked about his employment status in an interview for another hotel sales job. He answered bluntly, "I was fired."

When the stunned interviewer asked to hear more, Nick explained:

> *"My boss and I just didn't get along, and I have to admit I didn't handle the situation well. I certainly understand the importance of call reports and log sheets and other sales-management controls. I guess I interpreted some of Joe's quick demands for these things as a lack of trust, and I shouldn't have. I've learned my lesson."*

 GREEN LIGHT

Talk less about why you were terminated and more about what you've learned from the experience.

If you were laid off, or, as the British quaintly say, "made redundant," you shouldn't be expected to apologize. You might say something like, "Yes, I was one of 16 people laid off when sales took a slide." (This is an easy way out, presuming you were not a member of the sales department!)

RED LIGHT

As always, the introduction of any negative: "Yeah, I was fired because I'm not as young as I used to be. Wait until they see what my old lawyer has to say about age discrimination. I'll make them pay through the nose!"

Being fired for cause, especially if you refuse to admit responsibility or to detail what steps have been taken to correct the problem. Celebrity felons like Mike Tyson may get two or three or umpteen chances to make millions even after serving time, but most interviewers get a bit antsy about hiring someone who was fired for stealing, drinking on the job, hitting his or her boss, or some equally charming offense.

 DESCRIBE THE WAY YOUR DEPARTMENT IS ORGANIZED. ALSO, WHAT IS THE TITLE OF THE PERSON TO WHOM YOU REPORT? WHAT ARE HIS OR HER EXACT RESPONSIBILITIES?

 WHAT DO THEY WANT TO HEAR?

Did you hear that? If you've been vastly exaggerating the duties and responsibilities of your current position, that sound you heard was the door that just closed . . . behind you . . . on your way out of the interview.

This question is designed to clarify what you really do—how can you be doing "X" if you said that's your *boss's* main function?—and set up a series of follow-up questions about why you exaggerated (presuming the interviewer doesn't just say "thank you" then and there). Don't be surprised if you are asked to draw an organizational chart of your company or department.

GREEN LIGHT

Duties and responsibilities that match those claimed on your resume.

Duties and responsibilities commensurate with the job at hand.

An answer that is consistent with your answers to previous questions about work experience. The more detailed these answers, the easier it will be for an interviewer to catch any inconsistencies (at which point he or she will return to those previous answers and ask why the current one doesn't seem to mesh with them).

A clearly presented explanation of how your department, division, or company is set up, which tends to at least show consistency with your resume and implies that you have really done what you said you have. Be aware that a really good interviewer will take detailed notes so he can check each particular with your supervisor when he calls for a reference.

 RED LIGHT

A hazy, vague explanation that indicates you may be making it all up as you go along.

Glaring inconsistencies with your resume or previous answers.

Failure to include a key responsibility or job duty that was previously proclaimed, especially if it's one that is important to the new job.

An organizational plan that doesn't make sense to the interviewer. (The more experience you have at different companies, the more likely you will have been exposed to different structures and management styles, and the more confident you will feel that a structure that seems top heavy or one that gives lower-level staff members an extraordinary amount of freedom doesn't feel right.)

TELL ME ABOUT YOUR TYPICAL DAY AT YOUR CURRENT (LAST) JOB. HOW MUCH TIME DO YOU SPEND ON THE PHONE? IN MEETINGS? IN ONE-ON-ONE CHATS? WORKING BY YOURSELF? WORKING WITH YOUR TEAM (OR OTHERS)?

 WHAT DO THEY WANT TO HEAR?

Again, they are looking for the detail that will back up some of the earlier general statements you made (about responsibilities, duties, even favorite aspects of your job) or show that those statements were disingenuous or perhaps somewhat excessive.

VARIATIONS

- *On a typical day, tell me what you do in the first and last hour at work. When do you arrive and leave?*

- *Tell me what specific responsibilities you currently delegate. Are you delegating too many or too few tasks? Why? What's stopping you from changing this?*

- *How many hours per week do you have to work to fulfill your current responsibilities?*

- *What's the most important part of your current job to you? To your firm?*

 HOW LONG HAVE YOU BEEN LOOKING FOR A JOB?

 WHAT DO THEY WANT TO HEAR?

Unless you've been fired or laid off, your answer should always be that you've just started looking. If you think the interviewer has some way of finding out that you've been looking for a while (perhaps you've come to him through a recruiter who knows your history), be prepared to explain why you haven't received or accepted any offers.

Rightly or wrongly, many interviewers presume that the longer you've been out there, the less desirable you are to hire. Personally, I disagree. If someone's been looking for a month or two or three, are they inherently less desirable than a newly minted *ex*-employee who's still wearing his company T-shirt under his suit? It's unrealistic to expect that everyone who wants a job can find one right away. It's even less realistic not to assume that the most qualified candidates might well be picky and simply be ensuring a proper fit with the right company before plunging back into the corporate seas.

Nevertheless, be prepared to deal with those interviewers less understanding than I.

 ## WHY HAVEN'T YOU RECEIVED ANY OFFERS SO FAR?

 ## WHAT DO THEY WANT TO HEAR?

You're just as choosy about finding the right job as the interviewer is about hiring the right candidate. Don't whine or show that the search is upsetting you. If you've already fielded an offer or two, you might say,

> *"I have had an offer. But the situation was not right for me. I'm especially glad that I didn't accept, because I now have a shot at landing this position."*

It's important to tell the truth, however, because the interviewer's next logical questions may be the following:

WHO MADE YOU AN OFFER? FOR WHAT TYPE OF POSITION? AT WHAT SALARY?

 WHAT DO THEY WANT TO HEAR?

If you've already lied, you're in hot water now! Some interviewers will consider any admission of lying in these circumstances your "voluntary" offer to end the interview!

Many interviewers know a great deal about their competitors and which positions they're trying to fill. If you did the smart thing and told the truth, feel free to name the company.

It's important to stress that the position you turned down was very similar to the one you're applying for now. After all, if the job you are currently interviewing for is perfect for you—as you've undoubtedly already told the interviewer three or four times—why would you be at all interested in something very different at the other company?

 IF YOU DON'T LEAVE YOUR CURRENT JOB, WHAT WILL HAPPEN THERE? HOW FAR DO YOU EXPECT TO ADVANCE?

 WHAT DO THEY WANT TO HEAR?

Is desperation driving you away from your current job, so that you'll say or do anything to get this one? This doesn't exactly make you a prime candidate to most interviewers. Why should he or she save you?

Remember the adage, "There's no better time to look for a new job than when you're happy with your old one." Even if you'd rather hawk peanuts at the stadium than stay another month at ABC Widget, convince the interviewer that you're the type of employee who is capable of making the most of any situation, even an employment situation you've just said you want to leave.

You could say:

> *"Naturally I'm interested in this job and have been thinking about leaving ABC. However, my supervisors think highly of me, and I expect that one day other situations will open up for me at the company. I'm one of ABC's top salespeople. I have seen other people performing at similar levels advance to management positions. That's what I'm looking for right now."*

Whatever your feeling about your current job, it's always best to conduct your part of the interview as if you are in the driver's seat, just cruising along happily until you notice that a quick change of lanes would improve your career. You certainly aren't interested in getting off at the next exit, no matter where it leads!

Begin your answers with the phrase, "Well, assuming I'm not the successful candidate for this position. . . ." Without too much ego, let the interviewer know that you're taking your time. You're interested in choosing a job that's right for you.

 GREEN LIGHT

If you can claim (or do claim) that you will still advance and be given more responsibility, but perhaps at too slow a pace or without adequate compensation.

If you are able to describe a situation in which the company, through little or no fault of your own, will clearly not be able to keep or pay its top people what they're worth (for example, a pending merger, bankruptcy, cash flow problems, or loss of a key customer or product). Clearly, your reason for leaving is obvious and justifiable and your future there dim, through no fault of your own.

 RED LIGHT

"Well, I doubt I'll last the week. Old Scrawnynose will probably fire me right after lunch."

An answer that indicates problems at the company for which you must bear some responsibility. ("Well, sales are down 10 percent across the board, but my territory is down 72 percent. It's not *my* fault that all those stores went out of business!")

Although it's a good idea to convince your prospective employer that the world is your oyster—and you're simply waiting to find the perfect pearl of a job—you might get hit with questions like these:

 IF YOU'RE SO HAPPY AT YOUR CURRENT JOB, WHY ARE YOU LEAVING? WILL THEY BE SURPRISED?

 WHAT DO THEY WANT TO HEAR?

You may know your current company could go out of business at any second. Or you may be leaving because you just broke off your engagement with the person in the office next door. Don't cry on the interviewer's shoulder.

Instead, reassure him or her that you're not running away from anything. You've made the decision to move toward:

- More responsibility.

- More knowledge.

- The wonderful opportunity available at Good Times, Inc.

VARIATIONS

- *What would have to change at your current job to make it tenable?*

- *What have you had to change about yourself/your skills/philosophy/duties to adapt to changes at your current firm?*

- *What aspects of your current job were different than you expected when you took it?*

IF YOU HAVE THESE COMPLAINTS ABOUT YOUR CURRENT JOB/BOSS/COMPANY, AND THEY THINK SO HIGHLY OF YOU, WHY HAVEN'T YOU BROUGHT YOUR CONCERNS TO THEIR ATTENTION?

 WHAT DO THEY WANT TO HEAR?

The interviewer is trying to "hoist you by your own petard." Some problem solver you are! You can't even talk to your boss about changes that might make you happier!

If you do find yourself cornered, facing this dead end, the only way out is to be as positive as possible. Say something like:

> *"Grin & Bear It is aware of my desire to move up. But the company is still small. There's really not much they can do about it. The management team is terrific. There's no need right now to add to it, and they are aware of some of the problems this creates in keeping good performers. It's something they talk about quite openly."*

VARIATIONS

- *If you could eliminate one duty/responsibility from your current (last) job, what would it be and why?*

- *If you could make one comment or suggestion to your current boss, what would it be? Did you do anything of the sort? Why or why not?*

 HOW WOULD YOUR COWORKERS DESCRIBE YOU?

 WHAT DO THEY WANT TO HEAR?

Of course, they would describe you as an easy-going person who is a good team player. After all, you've found that "a lot more can be accomplished when people gang up on a problem, rather than on each other."

Once again, the personal inventory you completed in Chapter 1 will come in handy. Cull words from the lists you've titled "My strongest skills," "My greatest areas of knowledge," "My greatest personality strengths," and "The things I do best," and put them in the mouths of coworkers and friends.

VARIATIONS

- *What five adjectives would your last supervisor use to describe you?*

- *How effectively did your supervisor conduct appraisals?*

- *How did you do on your last performance appraisal?*

- *What were your key strengths and weaknesses cited by your supervisor?*

- *How did your last supervisor get the best performance out of you?*

- *What did you say and do the last time you were right and your boss was wrong?*

 GIVE ME SPECIFIC EXAMPLES OF WHAT YOU DID AT YOUR CURRENT (LAST) JOB TO INCREASE REVENUES/REDUCE COSTS/BE MORE EFFICIENT/SAVE EFFORT/ETC.

 WHAT DO THEY WANT TO HEAR?

This is a relative of the earlier questions you were asked about budgetary responsibility and how your current department is organized. (Savvy interviewers think it's a good idea after asking the first question or two to ask some different questions, *then* return to the subject later. Many candidates, having successfully navigated the shoals of the earlier questions, may be caught in an exaggeration when the interviewer returns to the question later on rather than following up on it immediately.)

 ## WHAT DO YOU FEEL AN EMPLOYER OWES AN EMPLOYEE?

 ## WHAT DO THEY WANT TO HEAR?

This is not—let me repeat, *not*—your invitation to discuss the employee benefits package you would like to have. It's a loaded question.

Don't get into a dissertation on the employer's moral responsibility to employees. For that matter, don't get into legal responsibilities. Try to refocus the interviewer's attention on your positive outlook, and keep your answer short and sweet:

> *"I think an employer owes its employees opportunity. In my next position, I look forward to the opportunity to run projects profitably."*

If the interviewer digs for a more specific response about a sensitive issue, such as your feelings about the information an employer should share with employees or the size of the raise pool, you could respond like this:

> *"I hope that my employer will be respectful of me as an employee and of any agreements we may negotiate in the course of business. However, I know that there are times when organizations face tough decisions that may require confidentiality and affect employees. That's business."*

THE SUCCESSFUL CANDIDATE FOR THIS POSITION
WILL BE WORKING WITH SOME HIGHLY TRAINED
INDIVIDUALS WHO HAVE BEEN WITH THE COMPANY
FOR A LONG TIME. HOW WILL YOU MESH WITH
THEM?

 WHAT DO THEY WANT TO HEAR?

Your answer should indicate your eagerness, as the new kid
on the block, to learn from your future coworkers. You don't
want to raise any doubts about how they might react to you.
Your answer may cite the skills, knowledge, and insights you
will add to the team, but it should stress that you have a lot
to learn from the people you'll be working with (even if, in
your heart of hearts, you think they're probably a bunch of
old fogies and you can't wait to get on board and shape
them up).

 YOUR SUPERVISOR TELLS YOU TO DO SOMETHING
IN A WAY YOU KNOW IS DEAD WRONG. WHAT
DO YOU DO?

 WHAT DO THEY WANT TO HEAR?

This is a tough question, so why not acknowledge it as such? Try
an answer like this:

> *"In such a situation, even the best employee runs
> the risk of seeming insubordinate. I would pose
> my alternative solution to my supervisor in the
> most deferential way possible. If he insisted
> that I was wrong, I guess I'd have to do it his
> way."*

IF YOU WERE UNFAIRLY CRITICIZED BY YOUR
SUPERVISOR, WHAT WOULD YOU DO?

 WHAT DO THEY WANT TO HEAR?

All of us can think back to a time when the pressure was on at
work and a mistake was made. Maybe you took more than your
fair share of the blame. Perhaps you were caught in circumstances beyond your control. In any event, your boss blamed
you. But chances are, you and your boss got through the rough
spot and you made sure the mistake never occurred again.

You could answer the question by telling of such an experience. You do not have to select the most vulnerable or perilous
moment of your career to illustrate the point. Simple mistakes
are more than adequate:

> *"In the course of my career there have been a few
> times when problems have come up and I have been
> held accountable for mistakes I did not feel I had
> caused. But a problem is a problem no matter who
> creates it, and you certainly don't have to create the
> problem to solve it. The most important thing is to
> deal with it.*
>
> *"On those occasions when the issue has been sig-
> nificant enough, I have explained my point of view
> to my supervisor later—after the situation has been
> resolved and the atmosphere has calmed."*

 WOULD YOU LIKE TO HAVE YOUR BOSS'S JOB? WHY
OR WHY NOT?

 WHAT DO THEY WANT TO HEAR?

No matter how you answer this question, the interviewer
will learn a lot about you, so proceed with caution. It's an

indirect way of finding out whether or not you want to be promoted.

Let's start with the first part of the question: Saying "yes" indicates you're ambitious and interested in career advancement. Saying "no" indicates doubts or reservations, at least about the job in question.

In the second part of the question, things get sticky. For instance, if it's clear that you're interested in promotion and the position you are applying for doesn't offer a direct path to a higher level, then the interviewer may conclude that you'll be disappointed. On the other hand, in a highly competitive organization, expressing reservations about career advancement could knock you out of the running immediately.

There are two things you should do to prepare for this question. First, in your preliminary research, get a sense of the corporate culture and opportunities for advancement. Try to be aware of the possibilities going into the interview.

Second, know what your honest answer to the question is. Maybe you're ready, willing, and anxious to move up and take on your boss's job. Or maybe you shudder at the thought of a management job where you'd have to deal with personnel issues. "Know thyself" on this one, because if you're hired, your answer may come back to haunt you.

Now put the results together to develop your response. Ideally, your honest answer will suit the company. If your aspirations are incompatible with the possibilities, you can—at your own risk—compensate by offering an answer that fits. No matter what, make it *positive:*

> *"In time, I would love to have my boss's job. I'm particularly interested in the vendor relationships and sales promotion sides of buying."*

> *"I am very interested in career advancement, but my current boss's responsibilities are heavily*

weighted toward managing department production. In time, I hope to move into a position with primary responsibility for design quality."

"I would be open to taking on additional responsibilities, but I like the autonomy of a sales position, and I find it rewarding to work directly with clients. My boss is mainly responsible for supervising the department and its personnel. In such a position, I would miss the client contact."

WHAT IF PIGS COULD FLY AND. . . .

Hypothetical ("what if . . . ?") questions are the basis of a situational interview, in which the interviewer conjures up a series of situations, real or imaginary, in order to ascertain whether you have the resourcefulness, logic, creativity, and ability to think under pressure. Why apply such pressure? Even the best-prepared candidates can't prepare for *these* questions!

Situational interview questions can come in any shape or style. I've given you only a handful of samples here. But once you get the idea, see if you can outsmart the interviewer. If you have a detailed description of the job you're applying for, use your imagination to try to anticipate a number of situations that might come up once you're behind the desk.

YOUR SUPERVISOR LEFT AN ASSIGNMENT IN YOUR IN-BOX, THEN WENT ON VACATION FOR THE WEEK. YOU CAN'T REACH HIM, AND YOU DON'T FULLY UNDERSTAND THE ASSIGNMENT. WHAT WOULD YOU DO?

The interviewer is attempting to gauge whether you have an appropriate respect for hierarchy and deadline demands. Alternatively, it may be a way for a more entrepreneurial firm to see whether you are willing to make decisions when forced to, even if, inevitably, mistakes will occur.

If there is truly no way to reach your boss or leave a message via voicemail or E-mail, you'd suck up the courage to approach your boss's supervisor.

Of course, you would do this in a way that would not reflect badly on your boss, explaining that you and your boss simply missed the chance to discuss the assignment before he had to leave the office. Because you're not yet familiar with the company's procedures, you simply want to be sure that you understand the assignment, so you can start on it as soon as possible.

 YOUR BEST FRIEND CONSTANTLY BORROWS MONEY FROM PETTY CASH AND FAILS TO RETURN IT. YOU'VE SPOKEN TO HER, AND SHE JUST LAUGHED AT YOU. WHAT DO YOU DO?

 WHAT DO THEY WANT TO HEAR?

That despite your feelings of friendship, the company comes first; you'd turn her in.

 IF I ASKED YOU TO PUT TOGETHER A FOCUS GROUP FOR A NEW PRODUCT WE'RE INTRODUCING, WHAT WOULD YOU DO?

 OUR SALESPEOPLE HAVEN'T MET QUOTA FOR THE LAST THREE QUARTERS. WHAT WOULD YOU DO?

 WHAT DO THEY WANT TO HEAR?

Questions, questions, and more questions. At least at the beginning. Then they want to "hear" your thought process as you figure out what you would do.

HOW TO SHINE IN ANY SITUATIONAL INTERVIEW

◉ **ADMIT THAT A TOUGH SITUATION WOULD MAKE YOU NER-VOUS.** You might even panic momentarily. No interviewer is looking for a candidate bent on plunging right in—and then flailing about without considering consequences or alternatives. Nervousness produces the adrenaline that often fuels creative strategies.

◉ **TAKE A MOMENT TO THINK BEFORE YOU ANSWER.** This shows you are not likely to plunge into any situation with a hotheaded response. Rather, you are taking the time to weigh alternatives and choose the best course of action.

◉ **AVOID THROWING THE "BULL."** No matter what the interview technique, quash the temptation to exaggerate or downright fabricate a response.

◉ **SHOW THAT YOU HAVE A GRASP OF THE REAL WORLD.** Admit that you have a lot to learn about this company and the position. This approach is far more effective than trying to sell yourself as a savior.

◉ **PLAN YOUR ANSWERS TO A NUMBER OF DIFFERENT SITUATIONS AHEAD OF TIME.** Assume that some of these questions will be about areas of knowledge and skill you have yet to develop, so learn as much as you can about what you don't know. And have a strategy for finding the information or resources you currently lack.

So Why Us?

In most prizefights, the first couple of rounds are relatively boring. The boxers spend their time checking each other out, testing each other's feints and jabs, before the real mayhem begins.

The same could be said of most interviews. After the first bell, the pleasantries begin. The second bell signals the getting-to-know-you round of questioning. Then, if the interviewer thinks it's worthwhile, he begins pummeling you . . . with questions meant to separate the stiffs from the real contenders.

If you've already confidently answered a dozen or so questions, you're in that pummeling stage. Your chance to dance around open-ended questions is long gone. In order to make it to the final bell, you need to demonstrate some real knowledge.

DO YOU KNOW MUCH ABOUT OUR COMPANY?

 WHAT DO THEY WANT TO HEAR?

Believe it or not, many candidates think this is merely an ice-breaker and simply answer, "No."

Don't you follow suit! After all, why would you go into one of the most important encounters of your life so thoroughly unprepared? And then admit it?

I have urged (okay, nagged) you to do your homework. This is where your research will come in handy. Toss out a few salient (and positive) facts about the company, then lob a question that demonstrates your interest back into the interviewer's court. For example:

> *"Boy, what a growth story Starter Up is! Didn't I read recently that you've had seven straight years of double-digit growth? I read in your annual report that you're planning to introduce a new line of products in the near future. I jumped at the chance to apply here. Can you tell me a little bit about this division and the position that's available?"*

 GREEN LIGHT

Any answer that demonstrates your preinterview research. The more informed you are, the more likely you will end up at the top of the list of potential employees.

A detailed answer that indicates the breadth of your research, from checking out the company's Internet site to reading its annual report and becoming familiar with its products and services. Referring to a trade magazine article that mentions the company or, better yet, the interviewer, is a nice touch, don't you think?

VARIATIONS

- *What do you know about the community (town, city) in which we're located?*

- *In which of our offices would you prefer to work?*

- *Would you have a problem traveling between a few of our offices?*

 DO YOU HAVE ANY QUESTIONS?

 WHAT DO THEY WANT TO HEAR?

Normally, this question occurs very near the conclusion of the interview. In fact, you may well assume that its appearance pretty much signals the end. Nevertheless, because we've been talking about the importance of your preinterview research, this is as good a place as any to address this question.

Never, I repeat, *never* answer with a "no." How can you make one of the most important decisions of your life—whether to work for this company at this job—without knowing more?

Even if you think you're sold on the position and clear on the responsibilities, you must speak up here. If you don't, the interviewer will assume you are uninterested. And that could be the kiss of death to you as an applicant, even at this late stage.

 WHAT DO *YOU* WANT TO KNOW?

It's easy to get caught up in the challenge of impressing the interviewer with your brilliant answers, but it's also important that you don't lose sight of the fact that you have a goal—trying to determine whether this situation is right for you, whether this job is worthy of your talents and commitment.

With this in mind, here are a few key questions I would want to ask:

> *"Can you give me a formal, written description of the position? I'm interested in reviewing in detail the major activities involved and what results are expected."*

This is a good question to pose to the screening interviewer. It will help you prepare to face the hiring manager. If a written description doesn't exist, ask the interviewer to dictate as complete a description of the job to you as possible.

> *"Does this job usually lead to other positions at the company? Which ones?"*

You don't want to find yourself in a dead-end job. So find out how you can expect to advance after you land this job. What happened to the person you would be replacing? Is he or she still with the company? If so, doing what?

Try to pursue this line of questioning without giving the impression that you can't wait to get out of a job you don't even have yet! If you ask such questions in a completely non-threatening manner, your ambition will be understood, even welcomed.

> *"Tell me some of the particular skills or attributes that you want in the candidate for this position."*

The interviewer's answer should tell you how much your traits are valued. With this information, you can emphasize those traits you possess at the close of the interview to end it on a strong note.

> *"Please tell me a little bit about the people with whom I'll be working most closely."*

I wish someone had told me about this question before my last job interview! The answer can tell you so many things, like how good the people you could be working with are at their jobs and how much you are likely to learn from them. Most important, you'll find out whether the hiring manager seems enthusiastic about his team.

A hiring manager usually tries to put on his best face during an interview, just as you do as the prospective candidate. But catching the interviewer off guard with this question can give you a glimpse of the real feelings hiding behind that "game face."

If she doesn't seem enthusiastic, you probably won't enjoy being part of her team. This particular hiring manager may attribute little success, and perhaps a lot of headaches, to the people who work for her.

"What do you like best about this company? Why?"

If the interviewer hems and haws a lot over this one, it may indicate that she doesn't really like the company that much at all.

If she's instantly enthusiastic, her answer should help sell you on her and the company.

The answer to this question can also give you a good sense of the values of the organization and the hiring manager. If she talks about nothing but products and how well her stock options are doing, it indicates a lack of enthusiasm for the people-side of the business.

"What is the company's ranking within the industry? Does this position represent a change from where it was a few years ago?"

You should already have some indication of the answer to this question from your initial research, particularly if the company is publicly owned. If you have some of this information, go ahead and build it into your question:

"I've read that the company has risen from fifth to second in market share in just the past three years. What are the key reasons for this dramatic success?"

This question again clearly illustrates that you have done your research . . . and are ready to flaunt it!

Do shy away from asking about days off, vacation, holidays, sick pay, personal days, and so on. You'll seem like someone who is looking for a chance to get out of the office before you even start!

Here's the most comprehensive list of questions I can devise. Again, attempt to gain answers to them before the interview (although this will not always be possible, especially if you are interviewing with a small, privately held company).

QUESTIONS ABOUT THE COMPANY

- What are the company's leading products or services? What products or services is it planning to introduce in the near future?

- What are the company's key markets, and are those markets growing?

- Will the company be entering any new markets in the next couple of years? Which ones and via what kind of distribution channel(s)?

- What growth rate are you currently anticipating? Will this be accomplished internally or through acquisitions?

- Who owns the company?

- Please tell me about your own tenure with the XYZ Company.

- How many employees work for the organization? In how many offices? In this office?

- Is the company planning to grow through acquisitions?

- What has been the company's layoff history in the last five years? Do you anticipate any cutbacks in the near future and, if you do, how will they impact my department or position?

- What major problems or challenges has the company recently faced? How were they addressed? What results do you expect?

- What is the company's share of each of its markets?

- Which other companies serving those markets pose a serious threat?

- Please tell me more about your training programs. Do you offer reimbursement for job-related education? Time off?

- What is your hiring philosophy?

- What are the company's plans and prospects for growth and expansion?

- What are the company's goals in the next few years?

- What do you like best about this company? Why?

- What is the company's ranking within the industry? Does this represent a change from where it was a year or a few years ago?

QUESTIONS ABOUT THE DEPARTMENT OR DIVISION

- Explain the organizational structure of the department and its primary functions and responsibilities.

- To whom will I be reporting? To whom does he or she report?

- With which other departments does this department work most closely?

- How many people work exclusively in this department?

- What problems is this department facing? What are its current goals and objectives?

QUESTIONS ABOUT THE JOB

- What kind of training should I expect and for how long?

- How many people will be reporting to me?

- Is relocation an option, a possibility, or a requirement?

- How did this job become available? Was the previous person promoted? What is his or her new title? Was the previous person fired? Why?

- Would I be able to speak with the person who held this job previously?

- Is a written job description available?

- Could you describe a typical day in this position?

- How long has this position been available?

- How many other candidates have you interviewed? How many more candidates will you be interviewing before you make a decision?

- Is there no one from within the organization who is qualified for this position?

- Before you're able to reach a hiring decision, how many more interviews should I expect to go through and with whom?

- Where will I be working? May I see my office/cubicle?

- How advanced/current is the hardware and software I will be expected to use?

- How much day-to-day autonomy will I have?

- Does this job usually lead to other positions in the company? Which ones?

- Please tell me a little bit about the people with whom I'll be working most closely.

 ## WHAT INTERESTS YOU MOST ABOUT THIS POSITION? OUR COMPANY?

 ## WHAT DO THEY WANT TO HEAR?

You know the drill from some of the previous chapters. You have your eye on more responsibility, more opportunities, the chance to supervise more people, and the chance to develop a new set of skills and sharpen the ones you've already acquired. And, of course, if they absolutely insist they'll increase your salary, well, you certainly aren't one to be negative and say no!

However, this is also the ideal time to demonstrate what you know about this company and how the position for which you're interviewing can contribute to its success.

 ## GREEN LIGHT

Armed with this knowledge, you might reply, "I've heard so much about your titanium ball bearings that I've wanted to experiment with different applications for them." Rather than, "I'll have a better commute if I get this job." (Unbelievably, I have heard this response from more than one candidate I've interviewed! It may be honest, even important to the candidate, but it sure wasn't the answer *I* wanted to hear!)

RED LIGHT

Be careful of any answer that clearly demonstrates incompatibility; if your primary interest lies in an area that will be peripheral, at best, to your real function, you're just setting yourself up for a "Thank you, we'll be in touch."

VARIATION

● *On a scale of one to five, rate your interest in this company. In this job.*

 WHAT HAVE YOU HEARD ABOUT OUR COMPANY THAT YOU DON'T LIKE?

 WHAT DO THEY WANT TO HEAR?

This is tricky. Obviously, you want to minimize the negative implications of any question, including this one. If there hasn't been any dire news, you could ask about the dearth of the most current software or express your wish that the company's profits were a bit more predictable.

Of course, the existence of real news changes your response. Maybe you've heard that ABC Widget had a layoff 12 months ago and you're wondering if the dust has settled yet. Or perhaps you've heard rumors of a merger.

Don't play dumb. Given either of the above scenarios, any new prospect would have reservations about the company's stability and plans for the future. If the interviewer opens the door for you to ask what might otherwise be uncomfortable questions, by all means walk right in.

Just don't slam it in your own face by raising a huge negative: "I'm not sure I like the fact that I'll be reporting to three different executives" or "Is it possible to be scheduled for a salary review in 30 days?"

THIS IS A MUCH LARGER (SMALLER) COMPANY
THAN YOU'VE WORKED FOR. HOW DO YOU FEEL
ABOUT THAT?

 WHAT DO THEY WANT TO HEAR?

If the company is larger, you are undoubtedly looking forward
to terrific growth opportunities and exposure to more areas of
knowledge than you have access to now.

If the prospective company is smaller, you are looking forward to a far less bureaucratic organization, where decisions can
be made much more quickly and where no department is so
large that its people are unfamiliar with the workings of the
entire company.

 WHAT ARE YOU LOOKING FOR IN YOUR NEXT JOB?

 WHAT DO THEY WANT TO HEAR?

Obviously, you should tailor your response to the job for which
you're applying. But answering with a slightly reorganized rendi-
tion of the job description isn't the right way to go about it.

Interviewers typically ask a question like this to gauge your
level of interest in the job and see if you have any doubts. So
focus on the job at hand. Think of key skills the job requires, and
emphasize your interest in having a chance to develop (or further develop) one of them. And don't forget to express enthusiasm for your field of work. Here is an example:

> *"In my current position as development research*
> *associate, I research corporate and government*
> *funding opportunities and write grant proposals.*
> *I enjoy my work very much, but my contact with*
> *prospective donors has been limited. I look forward*
> *to a position that offers more opportunities to work*

with donors, secure their support, and ensure that they are recognized for their contributions.

"I have had a few opportunities to do this with my current employer, and based on my success in dealing with Timely Donations, Inc., I know I can successfully advocate an organization's mission to gain needed corporate support."

VARIATIONS

- *If you could have any job in the world, what would it be?*

- *If you could work for any company in the world, which would it be?*

This is not the time to wax philosophic about your dreams, let alone your fantasies. You may well harbor a desire to work in Paris, but if the company with which you're interviewing doesn't happen to have an office in France, why are you bothering to bring it up?

On the other hand, disingenuously telling the interviewer that *his* is your dream company is not usually believable.

Since virtually any answer is just going to land you in the proverbial hot water, you'd do better to find a way to slide around the question as quickly as possible.

 WHAT ASPECT OF THE JOB I'VE DESCRIBED APPEALS TO YOU LEAST?

 WHAT DO THEY WANT TO HEAR?

Let me lead with a little humor. After conversing with his Irish friend one day, a man finally blurted out in consternation, "Why do the Irish always answer a question with a question?" Unruffled, the Irishman winked and replied, "Do we now?"

Your best tactic is to follow suit. Shoot the question right back at the interviewer! For example, you might say:

> *"You've described a position in which I'd be overseeing some extraordinary levels of output. What sort of quality-control procedures does this company have? Will I be able to consult with in-house specialists?"*

Much like the question asked earlier ("What have you heard about our company that you don't like?"), I would presume this question is inviting a real answer. If you aren't going to take the job (unbeknownst to the interviewer) because of what you believe to be a fundamental flaw in the job or the company, a good interviewer will want to know about it.

One of three possible scenarios will result:

- You'll reveal an objection that isn't valid. Once the interviewer answers it, you will again be an interested candidate.

- You'll reveal a viable objection that leads the interviewer to eliminate you from consideration.

- You'll reveal a viable objection that will lead you to remove *yourself* from consideration.

 BASED ON WHAT YOU KNOW ABOUT OUR INDUSTRY, HOW DOES YOUR IDEAL JOB STACK UP AGAINST THE DESCRIPTION OF THE JOB FOR WHICH YOU'RE APPLYING?

 WHAT DO THEY WANT TO HEAR?

The ideal job is always one in which you'll have a broad scope of responsibilities that will enable you to continue to learn about your industry and enhance your skills. So use your knowledge about the industry to formulate a reply that, though perhaps a bit idealistic, doesn't sound unrealistic:

> *"I know that many accounting firms are deriving more and more of their fee income from consulting services. I'd like a job that combines my cost-accounting expertise with client consultation and problem solving. Ideally, I'd like to start as part of a team, then eventually head up a practice in a specific area, say, cost accounting in manufacturing environments."*

Now, based on what you know about the position, touch on one (and only one) minor shortcoming, and formulate a few careful questions about some aspects of the position you don't know about. Expanding on the above example, you might say:

> *"I know this position is in the auditing area and that you hire many of your entry-level people into that department. I must confess, I would like this to be a stepping stone to working more in the manufacturing area and, several years down the line, in consulting. I'm sure I don't have the requisite knowledge or experience yet. Is this a position in which I can gain such experience, and is this a career track that's possible at this firm?"*

 HOW WILL YOU HANDLE THE LEAST INTERESTING OR MOST UNPLEASANT PARTS OF THIS JOB?

 WHAT DO THEY WANT TO HEAR?

An interviewer posing this question usually will build in specific aspects of the position, such as, "You won't always be looking for creative solutions to our clients' tax problems. Most of the time, you'll be churning out returns and making sure you comply with the latest laws. You're aware of that, of course?" You might answer:

> *"I'm sure that every job in the accounting field has its routine tasks. They have to be done, too. Doing those tasks is part of the satisfaction of doing the job well. They make the relatively infrequent chances we have to be creative even more satisfying."*

 YOU'VE HAD LITTLE EXPERIENCE WITH BUDGETING (OR SALES OR WHATEVER). HOW DO YOU INTEND TO LEARN WHAT YOU NEED TO KNOW TO PERFORM ON THIS JOB?

 WHAT DO THEY WANT TO HEAR?

> *"Well, throughout my career, I've proven to be a quick study. For example, when my company's inventory system was computerized, I didn't have the time to go through the training. But the company that supplied the software had developed some computer-based tutorials and training manuals. I studied them and practiced at home. I hope that I'd be able to do something similar to pick up the rudiments of your budgeting system."*

You could also mention other options, such as learning from professional publications and seminars. The interviewer wants to be sure you won't just be sitting around twiddling your thumbs and complaining that you don't know what to do next. Reassure him or her that you plan to do whatever it takes to go right on learning throughout your tenure.

Now, how would you step in and save the day? If you don't know as much as you'd like about the position for which you're interviewing, spend some time with industry and trade publications. Focus on articles written to help people in this type of position solve common problems or those that suggest tips, tricks, and tools designed to increase everyday efficiency.

You want to demonstrate that you're ready to step right in and handle a tough situation with a cool head.

It's also a good idea to sharpen your working knowledge and skills. Interviewers like to pose problems you can solve on the spot. These exercises are intended to demonstrate your proficiency in the areas most important to the job.

Preparation makes perfect. If you come up blank, or use a fact or formula inaccurately during one of these exercises, it will be difficult, if not impossible, to recoup your credibility. That would be especially unfortunate after you've gotten this far.

Caveat: Different companies may use slightly different terms for the same procedure or material. So explain your terminology up front to make sure you're communicating clearly.

 ## HOW LONG DO YOU PLAN TO STAY WITH US?

 ## WHAT DO THEY WANT TO HEAR?

One answer I don't want to hear is "forever," because I simply won't believe it (and I'll wonder about the intelligence of a candidate who would think that's what I want to hear). You should offer a fairly simple answer along the lines of "as long as I continue to grow, continue to learn, and continue to contribute in ways you feel are valuable."

I'm not sure whether this question will ever give an interviewer any useful information, because any candidate candid (or stupid) enough to blurt out "oh, a month or two, until I find a job I really like" shouldn't have made it through the screening process (or, for that matter, the first 10 questions of the interview). But be careful your body language doesn't reveal your real answer. Squirming *does* imply, "oh, a month or two, until I find a job I really like"!

If you already appear to be a job-hopper but trot out the standard "as long as I continue to grow, etc." speech, don't be surprised if the interviewer asks, "Is that what you told the interviewers at your four previous positions?" Whatever you do, don't answer, "Yep, and they all believed me, too!"

 HOW DO YOU THINK I'VE HANDLED THIS INTERVIEW?

 WHAT DO THEY WANT TO HEAR?

Well, your options aren't very pleasant, are they? Saying "lousy" doesn't seem appropriate, but "great, sir, and may I polish your shoes?" seems a bit too obsequious. There is no right answer, much like the hypothetical questions in a situational interview, so don't offer one—ask a question of your own instead.

 LET'S GET PERSONAL

Most people think that the candidate who talks only about work, work, work stands the best chance of getting the job. But there's a "you" that exists after 5 p.m., and most interviewers want to get to know that person, too.

The guiding principle for answering personal questions is the same as it is for responding to queries about your professional experiences: Emphasize the positive. Let the interviewer in on the best and most interesting aspects of your personality.

Just be careful of saying too much. Your answers can reveal more information than the interviewer is entitled by law to ask for. For example, in the warm glow of an interview that seems to be going well, you might feel comfortable talking about your children and the challenges of being a single parent.

The interviewer could not have asked about your family situation in order to eliminate you from the running. Yet once this information has been revealed, it's fair game. He or she is free to use it to make unfair judgments about your ability to handle various aspects of the job. If the job you're applying for involves occasional overnight travel, for example, he or she may decide your family situation would create unnecessary difficulties.

So, while these questions do give you an opportunity to demonstrate what a terrific person you are, they could also prompt you to unwittingly provide information that dooms your candidacy! Make sure to study Chapter 9 to identify questions that are, at best, inappropriate and, at worst, illegal.

TO YOUR GOOD HEALTH

Employers have more than just a passing interest in your health. Most companies are looking for ways to keep the overall cost of healthcare insurance from skyrocketing. Most managers want to know that you won't be felled by every flu bug that makes the rounds and on sick leave when they need you most.

ARE YOU IN GOOD HEALTH? WHAT DO YOU DO TO STAY IN SHAPE?

You must be honest in answering this one. Prospective employers can find ways to check your medical history if they're worried about your health. In fact, many employers make job offers contingent on your passing a physical examination.

If you appear to be dedicated to maintaining your own good health, you'll ease many of their concerns. You don't have to be an exercise nut. Just play up any activities you do regularly that provide at least some health benefit, such as yard work, home repairs, or just walking the dog.

DO YOU HAVE ANY PHYSICAL PROBLEMS THAT MAY
LIMIT YOUR ABILITY TO PERFORM THIS JOB? IF SO,
WHAT ACCOMMODATIONS WOULD BE NECESSARY?

This is a perfectly legitimate question for the interviewer to ask.
So be honest. Are you applying for a job that requires a lot of
data entry despite the fact that you've been waging an ongoing
battle with carpal tunnel syndrome? Will a lot of walking and
standing on the job trigger that problem knee?

Remember, though, the key words are "ability to perform
this job." A physical problem that is not job-related is not
pertinent . . . and none of the employer's business, by law.

 HOW DO YOU MANAGE TO BALANCE CAREER
AND FAMILY?

 WHAT DO THEY WANT TO HEAR?

Gosh, you are facing one tricky devil. Again, this is a perfectly
legal question, but it does make it decidedly difficult if you are
determined to keep any discussion of family out of the interview. Why would you want to avoid such a discussion? If you've
been around the block a few times, you may legitimately worry
that the interviewer has some unwritten rules, such as no single
parents hired for travel positions (or, for that matter, no parents
if travel exceeds "X" percent).

Accordingly, if you're attempting to give an answer that is as
unrevealing as possible, try something like this:

> *"I have been a dedicated, loyal, hardworking*
> *employee throughout my career and nothing in my*
> *personal life—family obligations, hobbies, or*
> *volunteer work—has ever affected my performance.*
> *Nor would I ever expect it to."*

WHAT DO YOU LIKE TO DO WHEN YOU'RE NOT AT WORK?

 ## WHAT DO THEY WANT TO HEAR?

Many employers subscribe to the theory "If you want something done, give it to a busy person." So, you want to portray yourself as an active, vital individual. Take this opportunity to paint a self-portrait of a well-rounded person.

Be sure to emphasize those activities that may complement your on-the-job duties. For example, if you're applying for a position as a bookstore manager, mentioning that you read three books a week is highly appropriate. Your addiction to helicopter skiing probably isn't (for any job!).

VARIATIONS

- *What are your hobbies?*

- *What turns you on in your off-hours?*

 ## GREEN LIGHT

Shy away from the controversial. A savvy candidate will cite "reading" and "tennis," for example, rather than "bungee jumping," "picketing abortion clinics," or "raising money for the Liberal Party." Do you really want your off-hours interests to come between you and the job you're after? Then don't brag about activities that could cause a squeamish employer to envision a prolonged sick leave or ongoing legal problems.

It's generally safe to talk about most sports activities— participating in team sports; coaching children; or indulging in singular activities such as swimming, running, walking, or bicycling. Avoid emphasizing activities that are likely to spark concern or controversy, such as skydiving or hunting.

As a rule, employers like activities that show you are community minded and people oriented. Your involvement with the chamber of commerce, Toastmasters, the Rotary Club, or fundraising for charities is likely to earn points. However, avoid mentioning any religious or political activities that may alienate the interviewer. Carefully craft your answer so you don't:

- Sound like a couch potato. "I'm a Giants fan. I never miss a game. I also catch every episode of *The OC, 24,* and *One Tree Hill.* And I tape my soap operas every afternoon so I can catch up on them on the weekends."

- Seem headed for a collapse. "I play racquetball, coach a softball team, am on the board of directors of the local museum, plan to run for city council this fall, and, in my spare time, attend lectures on Egyptology at the university." (Whew! How will you find the time and energy for work?)

- Boast about dangerous activities. "I like to challenge myself. Next weekend, I'm signed up for another parachute jump. I need something to keep me pumped up until rugby season starts."

- Bring up controversial interests that may be personally objectionable to the interviewer. "I'm always on the front lines at Greenpeace demonstrations." Or "I give all my money to the Crusade to Convert the World to (fill-in-the-blank) religion."

TIPS FOR TOOTING YOUR OWN HORN—WITHOUT BECOMING A "BLOW-HARD"

○ **DON'T GET CARRIED AWAY.** Only the most annoying people don't find it difficult to talk about themselves in a flattering way. And that's what you'll be doing on the interview—constantly tooting your own horn, until even you will want to change the tune.

○ **STRESS THE TRAITS COMPANIES ARE LOOKING FOR.** I mean enthusiasm, confidence, energy, dependability, and honesty. Formulate answers that suggest these characteristics. Think about what you would want in an ideal employee if you owned a company. Wouldn't you want a problem solver? A team player? Someone who is enthusiastic about working hard to achieve goals?

○ **BE CREATIVE.** A friend of mine had to work his way through college. Rather than participate in low- or no-pay internship programs or extracurricular activities, he pumped gas and stocked supermarket shelves during the summer. So when asked why he hadn't had any internships, he was ready to reply:

> *"I wish I'd had more time to write for the school paper. Whenever I wasn't studying, I pretty much had to work to pay for college. But I learned a number of things from the jobs I held that most people learn only after they've been in their careers for a while, such as how to work with other people and how to manage my time effectively."*

MORE TIPS FOR INTERVIEW SUCCESS

⦿ **SHAPE YOUR RESPONSES TO THE POSITION.** Learn as much as you can about the position for which you are interviewing **before** you get to the interview. When you highlight your accomplishments, skills, and experience, relate them to the company's needs, wants, and goals.

⦿ **THINK IN TERMS OF WHAT . . . AND WHY.** As you trumpet your successes—or mumble about your failures—stress the positive lessons you learned from each situation and how you've already applied them (or plan to in your next position).

⦿ **DON'T EXAGGERATE.** Your accomplishments and responsibilities should speak for themselves. If you felt you lacked opportunities to make a mark in a past position, say so. But don't bend the truth; there are too many ways a savvy interviewer can find you out. Don't learn this lesson the hard way—it will probably cost you the job!

⦿ **DON'T APPEAR DESPERATE . . .** even if your last job was months ago. Some interviewers will equate "desperate" with "cheap to hire," presuming they want to hire you at all. But don't come across as smug, either. Concentrate on expressing your genuine interest and enthusiasm for the opportunities inherent in the job on offer.

⦿ **AVOID THE NEGATIVE.** You want the interviewer to associate nothing but positive words, thoughts, and deeds with you.

- **MAKE THE BEST OF YOUR CURRENT POSITION.** Convey that you are a positive person who always makes the best of *any* situation. The worse your actual situation, the better you'll look.

- **BUILD A VOCABULARY OF ACTION WORDS** and use them consistently in your resume, cover letter, follow-up letters, and during interviews. (See p. 174 for a full list.)

WORDS THAT PACK A PROFESSIONAL PUNCH

Ability	Discovered	Operated
Accelerated	Disproved	Organized
Accomplished	Effective	Persuaded
Accurate	Eliminated	Planned
Achieved	Enlarged	Prepared
Adjusted	Established	Presented
Administered	Evaluated	Processed
Advised	Examined	Produced
Analyzed	Excelled	Proficiency
Approved	Expanded	Programmed
Arranged	Focused	Promoted
Calculated	Formulated	Provided
Capable	Founded	Recommended
Communicated	Generated	Reduced
Compiled	Guided	Reorganized
Completed	Identified	Researched
Conceived	Implemented	Restored
Conceptualized	Improved	Reviewed
Conducted	Increased	Revised
Consolidated	Initiated	Scheduled
Constructed	Installed	Solved
Consulted	Instituted	Streamlined
Controlled	Instructed	Strengthened
Coordinated	Introduced	Supervised
Counseled	Invented	Systematic
Created	Launched	Tested
Decreased	Led	Thorough
Delivered	Maintained	Trained
Designed	Managed	Translated
Detected	Modified	Updated
Determined	Monitored	Utilized
Developed	Motivated	Vital
Directed	Negotiated	Won

Innocent? Hardly.
Illegal? Maybe.

As the head of recruiting for a rather large company, a friend of mine spent weeks at a time interviewing scores of candidates for a wide variety of openings. With so much practice, she became very good at identifying unsuitable candidates in minutes—and "releasing" the unsuspecting person with a simple "'Thanks for stopping by" before the interview even got underway!

Here's how it worked: On greeting a young applicant for a field sales position one morning, my friend asked, "How are you?" The applicant immediately began whining that it was raining and she had a run in her stocking.

This was a cue to my friend. She turned to the candidate and, feigning embarrassment, said, "Oh! Are you here to apply for that field sales position? I'm sorry. We forgot to call. We filled the position yesterday. But we'll keep you in mind for other, similar positions that come along. Thanks for stopping by."

DON'T "THROWAWAY" YOUR CHANCES

This story demonstrates a fact that few candidates realize: There is no such thing as an innocent or throwaway question. You are being judged from the moment the interviewer sees you (or hears you on the telephone) until the instant you are offered the job (or escorted out of the building). Many interviewers use these questions as ice-breakers, believing that they give a false, informal impression of "let's just chat, shall we?" and lead candidates to drop their interview guard. Some interviewees, dismissed after only a few minutes, belatedly discover that these innocent questions "ice-picked" their chances for the job.

The following are a few such questions to prepare for.

 HOW ARE YOU TODAY?

 WHAT DO THEY WANT TO HEAR?

You're doing just fine, thank you. And no, you didn't have any trouble at all! That's because (don't admit to this, just do it) you took the time to get directions from the interviewer's assistant.

Again, it all comes down to being positive. I'm not suggesting that you plaster an idiot grin on your face and blather like a "Stepford" employee. But I do urge you to make every effort not to let anything negative (even the crummy weather!) enter into any part of your interaction with the interviewer.

Since my recruiter friend told me his little story, I know I pay much more attention to the answers candidates give to these little throwaway questions.

VARIATIONS

- *Did you have any trouble finding us?*
- *Where are you staying? Do you like the hotel?*
- *How was your flight?*

WHAT'S THE LAST BOOK YOU READ?

 WHAT DO THEY WANT TO HEAR?

What someone chooses to read speaks volumes about what kind of a person he or she is. But before you reel off your reading list, consider this: Rightly or wrongly, many interviewers think that people who read nonfiction are more interested in the world than fiction readers, who are (they assume) just looking for an escape.

So rather than talk about the latest thriller you couldn't put down, opt for a popular business or motivational how-to book. This will demonstrate that you're interested in *The 7 Habits of Highly Effective People* or *The Discipline of Market Leaders* and trying to improve your knowledge and skill as a businessperson.

 WHAT'S THE LAST MOVIE YOU SAW?

 WHAT DO THEY WANT TO HEAR?

Mention a popular but uncontroversial movie. It won't do you any good to gleefully admit it was *Friday the 13th, Part 86*.

Do you want your taste in foreign films or left-wing documentaries to stand between you and a job? It's much better to stay with a Tom Hanks movie like *Forrest Gump*. (If you insist your preferences shouldn't matter, feel free to discuss your critiques of *Natural Born Killers* or *Pulp Fiction*.)

VARIATIONS

- *What three people would you most like to have dinner with?*

- *What other person would you invite to a desert island?*

- *What's your favorite book?*

- *Who's your favorite author?*

- *Who's your favorite actor?*

- *What's your favorite movie?*

- *What's your favorite TV show?*

- *What magazines do you read regularly?*

- *Where do you get your news?*

DISCRIMINATE AND ELIMINATE?

In an ideal world, companies and managers would judge every applicant solely on the basis of the skills and experience necessary to perform the job.

But it should come as no surprise that our world is far from ideal. In the real world, many managers and companies discriminate against people of color, people with disabilities, people over the age of 50, and even women, whom they may simply assume are planning to have children sometime during their future employment!

Few of us can claim to be completely objective when judging other people. But the fact is that you, as a candidate for any job, do not have to answer questions related to your race, nationality, marital or financial status—or even a disability if it is unrelated to how well you are able to perform the job.

ILLEGAL . . . OR JUST "INAPPROPRIATE"?

If an interviewer is foolish enough to make an issue of your nationality, marital status, or other personal information, should you leap out of your chair and make a citizen's arrest right there in his office? No.

But you should sit up and take notice. Every state has regulations governing what may and may not be asked of an applicant during the preemployment (application and interviewing) process. Just asking the wrong question is not illegal in itself. But it may open an employer up to a lawsuit if an otherwise-qualified applicant is passed over for a job based on his or her answer. Few companies are willing to take that chance. So when it comes to inappropriate questions, most employers tread lightly.

But regulations don't preclude the subtle techniques some interviewers use to get applicants to volunteer information. As an applicant, it's still up to you to dodge the bullet. The key is knowing when a question is inappropriate and then not surrendering any information that might cost you the job.

Every question the interviewer asks should pass this test: Does it have something to do with your current job or the one for which you're applying?

Beyond that, it pays to check with your state's Fair Employment Practices Commission for a list of questions considered inappropriate for employers to ask on job applications and during preemployment interviews.

In the meantime, here are some questions that should trigger alarms in your head during even the most congenial interview.

 ## HOW OLD ARE YOU?

Age can be a loaded issue for many employers. If you're in your late 40s or 50s, some employers may worry about your energy flagging or your health failing. Don't give them ammunition by confirming your age.

Employers cannot ask for your birth date or about facts that might reveal your age, such as the year you graduated from high school. Interviewers may only state that hiring is subject to verification of legal minimum-age requirements and that employees under the age of 18 must provide a work permit. (So asking whether you are at least 18 years old is a legal question.)

But age, like race, can be easy to guess. So again, take a positive tack. Play up the benefits of your experience and assure the employer that you have all the vitality for work you had when you were in your 20s. You might say,

> *"The more I've accomplished, the more effective I've become. When I was just starting out, I was so full of energy I was like a loose cannon. Now I find I can accomplish more in less time because I know where to find the resources I need and how to work effectively with all kinds of people."*

VARIATIONS

- *When were you born?*

- *When did you graduate from high school?*

- *When did you graduate from college?*

- *Are you near retirement age?*

- *Aren't you a little young to be seeking a job with this much responsibility?*

- *Aren't you a little too old for a fast-charging company such as ours?*

 ## ARE YOU SINGLE (MARRIED, SEPARATED, DIVORCED)?

An interviewer's bias may not be overt. Many interviewers use subtle ploys designed to get you to volunteer exactly the information that they then use to disqualify you from the running.

You may be married with children and proud of it. But resist the temptation to whip out the latest pictures from Walt

Disney World. Why? After all, what could seem more innocent than chitchatting about your girlfriend, spouse, or kids? What's the harm in letting an employer know about your tentative plan for having a child within a year?

Maybe there's no harm in it. But you never know how an interviewer may interpret your answers. If you're planning to have a child within a year, for example, an interviewer may worry about losing you for two, three, or more months. If you're engaged to be married, he might assume that you will be so wrapped up in wedding plans that your attention won't be focused on the job at hand.

Interviewers may not ask about your marital status or plans for marriage or for having children. If you already have children, you're not obliged to reveal their ages or the arrangements you've made for childcare. In many states, married women are not required to furnish their maiden name, unless they've worked under another name at previous companies listed on their resume.

You may be asked whether you are able and willing to relocate, to travel extensively, or to work overtime as needed (as long as the latter two questions are asked of all candidates). While these may be veiled attempts to discover whether you have a lot of family obligations—there may not actually *be* much travel or overtime—they are still legal questions, and you will need to have answers ready.

MEETING THE INTERVIEWER HALFWAY

Rather than simply refusing to answer a question and creating bad feelings between you and the interviewer, you may find it helpful to confront what appear to be the employer's concerns about your situation. For example, if the interviewer keeps digging for information about whether you have children, or plan to, he may be concerned about your commitment to the job. You might respond by saying something like:

> *"I sense that you are concerned about my ability to be here on a regular basis to put in the work necessary to meet deadlines. Just let me assure you that I have always been a reliable worker who's committed to getting the job done well and on time. In fact, in my last position, I was never late to work once, and I consistently completed all projects ahead of deadline."*

See? Without answering any questions about children or family plans, you addressed the real issue—the employer's concern about your commitment to your job.

VARIATIONS

- *What do you think caused your divorce?*

- *Why have you never married?*

- *Were you ever married?*

- *Do you intend to marry?*

- *Do you live alone?*

- *Do you have any children?*

- *Do you prefer to be called Miss, Ms., or Mrs.?*

- *Are you a single parent?*

- *How many dependents are you responsible for?*

- *Who's the boss in your family?*

- *What kind of work does your spouse do?*

- *How much time do you spend with your family?*

- *What do you think makes a happy marriage?*

- *Tell me about your children.*

- *Do you have a good relationship with your children?*

- *Do you have any children not living with you?*

- *Do you live with your parents?*

- *What childcare arrangements have you made for your children?*

- *My darn kids seem to pick up every bug that comes around. Yours, too?*

- *My wife (husband) hates me working on weekends. What about yours?*

- *Do you practice birth control?*

- *Are you pregnant?*

- *Do you intend to have children?*

- *Will travel be a burden on your family?*

- *Are you a family man (woman)?*

 ## WHAT'S YOUR NATIONALITY?

When you meet, you can't stop an interviewer from drawing conclusions about your lineage from the color of your skin, eyes, or hair. But never surrender that information over the telephone or hand over a photograph of yourself before you accept a job.

Employers may not ask about your ancestry, descent, parentage, or nationality, or that of your parents or spouse. It's okay to volunteer that you're proficient in a language other than English, but the interviewer cannot ask you how you learned to read, write, or speak that language.

Let's say your last name is obviously Italian. When you greet the interviewer, he remarks, "Rutigliano. That's Italian, isn't it?" What do you do? Just smile politely . . . and don't answer at all. It is quite possible that the interviewer meant absolutely no offense.

If the interviewer still doesn't get the hint and continues to allude to your Italian heritage, you might say, "I really don't see what my ancestry has to do with my application for this job." If you try to handle the situation diplomatically, you can stay on the interviewer's "good" side.

If an employer tries to pressure you into submitting a photograph of yourself to accompany your job application, simply say, "I don't have a suitable photograph available at this time. Of course, if I'm offered this job, I'd be happy to have one taken."

The Federal Immigration Reform and Control Act of 1986 prohibits employers from hiring illegal aliens—people who are not properly authorized to work in this country. So confirming that you *are* authorized to work in the U.S. is perfectly legitimate. In fact, once you have accepted the offer, you will be required to document your right to work by surrendering one of the following:

- A United States passport.

- A green card.

- A combination of a birth certificate or social security card and a driver's license.

VARIATIONS

- *Hmm, that's a/an ____ (Italian, Greek, etc.) name, isn't it?*

- *What language do you speak at home?*

- *Where are your parents from?*

- *Where were you born?*

● *Where were your parents born?*

● *What's your maiden name?*

● *Is that the last name you were born with?*

● *What languages do your parents speak?*

● *What do your parents do?*

● *Were your parents born in this country?*

● *Were you born in this country?*

● *What kind of accent is that?*

● *What languages do you speak?*★

● *Are you bilingual?*★

★This is a legal question if proficiency in one or more foreign languages is a requirement of the job.

 WHAT'S YOUR SEXUAL ORIENTATION?

"I'm sorry. I don't intend to discuss that."

VARIATIONS

● *Are you straight?*

● *Are you gay?*

● *Are you a lesbian?*

● *Do you date other men?*

● *Do you date other women?*

● *Do you have any roommates?*

● *Do you belong to any gay or lesbian groups?*

ARE YOU ____ (JEWISH, CHRISTIAN, BUDDHIST, ETC.)?

Employers may tell you which religious holidays the company observes. But they cannot ask you for any specific information in this area.

If an interviewer presses you to reveal your affiliation, simply say something like this:

> *"I like to keep my religious beliefs separate from my work, and I respect that right in the people with whom I work."*

But if you find yourself dodging too many of these "bullets," maybe you should take a moment to think about whether you want to work for a supervisor who has shown himself to be ignorant and insensitive. If you don't care that he's an insensitive boob—you just want the job—then don't make an issue out of his comments. It's up to you.

VARIATIONS

- *What do you do Sunday mornings?*
- *Can you work Friday evenings?*
- *We're a ____ (Christian, Jewish, Muslim) firm. Would that be a problem for you?*
- *Are you a member of any religious group?*
- *What religion do you practice?*
- *Do you tithe?*
- *Are you "born again"?*
- *Do your children go to Sunday School?*
- *Do your children go to Hebrew School?*

- *Do you sing in the church choir?*

- *What church do you belong to?*

- *Is there any day of the week on which you can't work?*

- *Will working on weekends be a problem for you?*

- *What religious holidays will you need to take?*

- *What organizations do you belong to?*

- *Have you ever done any missionary work?*

 DO YOU HAVE ANY PHYSICAL PROBLEMS?

Interviewers may only ask about a physical or mental disability *that will directly affect your performance on the job.*

Your general physical health is not fair game, although you may be asked to take a physical examination after you receive an offer. The outcome of this examination must be related to essential functions of the job, so the employer has the right to condition the offer on the results.

Employers may not ask about whether you have:

- An existing mental condition.

- Received workers' compensation.

- Problems with alcohol or drugs.

- HIV, AIDS, or AIDS-related syndrome.

 A WORD ABOUT AIDS

This is still an area of concern for employers. Although new laws and regulations will likely be written, HIV infection, AIDS, and AIDS-related medical conditions are currently considered "disabilities" under the Federal Americans with Disabilities Act.

If you test positive for HIV or AIDS (or any other disability) in a preemployment medical examination, the employer cannot use that information as grounds for withdrawing the offer *unless the extent of the illness substantially inhibits your ability to do the job or poses a reasonable threat to the safety of others in the workplace.*

VARIATIONS

- *Do you have any health problems?*

- *How many days were you sick last year?*

- *Do you spend a lot on prescriptions?*

- *Can you read the fine print on this form?*

- *How's your back?*

- *Is your hearing good?*

- *Were you ever denied health insurance?*

- *Were you ever denied life insurance?*

- *When were you last in the hospital?*

- *When did you last consult a doctor?*

- *Do you have a doctor you see regularly?*

- *Are you handicapped?*

- *Have you ever filed a worker's compensation claim?*

 WHAT ORGANIZATIONS DO YOU BELONG TO?

Think carefully about your answer to this question. An employer can ask about (and should only be interested in) your membership in organizations, professional societies, or other associations considered important to your performance on the job.

It's a good idea to leave out the names of any organizations that might provide clues to your race, religious creed, color, national origin, ancestry, gender, or disability.

 ## HAVE YOU EVER GONE BANKRUPT?

A prospective employer may only ask what you're currently earning.

Your current or past assets, liabilities, or credit rating are not fair game. This includes whether you own a home or any information about a past bankruptcy or garnishment of wages (except when permitted by federal and state laws governing credit-related information). Again, it's wise to consult the specific guidelines in your state.

VARIATIONS

- *Do you own or rent your home?*

- *Do you have any outside income?*

- *Do you earn any money from hobbies or investments?*

 ## WHAT WAS YOUR RECORD IN THE MILITARY?

If you have served in the military and want to bring to light the skills and knowledge you gained from that experience that are relevant to the job you're applying for, go ahead. But be aware that you're not required to give the dates of your military service or the type of discharge you received.

A dishonorable discharge from the military or an arrest that did not result in a conviction does not mean your professional life is over. In the majority of cases, these facts should remain in your past.

Be aware, however, that regulations do differ from state to state and from industry to industry. For example, under the Federal Deposit Insurance Act, banks are prohibited from hiring individuals convicted of any crime involving dishonesty or breach of trust, even if the conviction is more than seven years old.

VARIATION

- *What kind of discharge did you receive from the military?*

 HAVE YOU EVER BEEN ARRESTED?

Unless you're applying for a position as a police officer or with the Department of Justice, a prospective employer is not entitled to know whether you've been arrested unless the arrest resulted in a conviction.

In some states, employers may only ask about felonies, not misdemeanors. If you have a record, do some research.

 SO WHAT DO YOU DO?

Over the past 25 years, there has been a plethora of lawsuits charging employers with discriminatory hiring practices, yet inappropriate questions still are commonly asked during interviews. This is particularly true of interviews by hiring managers, who may not be "up to speed" on legal issues. If you're asked an inappropriate question, you have four choices:

- You can choose to answer the question, assuming that (for now, at least) the interviewer is not being wily, just curious.

- You can choose to answer the question you think the interviewer is *really* asking. He may not really care if you have kids, for example, if you point out that travel and overtime are no problem.

- You can make sure the interviewer is aware— oh so tactfully!—that he is treading on thin legal ice: "I'm not sure my religion is relevant to the job, but as you can see from my resume. . . . "

- You can end the interview. I'm presuming you are doing this because the interviewer has not stopped with one question, despite your tactful comment, but has continued to ask inappropriate questions. Why would you want to work in a company that has made it clear they discriminate?

▮ WHAT TO DO AFTER THE FACT

If an interviewer has asked you questions not related to the job on offer, and you believe you weren't hired based on your refusal to answer or the information you did provide, you might have grounds for charging the employer with discrimination.

The operative word here is "might." The burden of proof is on you. You will have to prove that the questions were asked for the purpose of discriminating among applicants. For example, if the manager asking all those questions about Italian ancestry subsequently hired another Italian, you wouldn't have much of a claim, despite the fact that you were asked inappropriate questions.

If you do think that you have grounds for a charge of discrimination, you should file your charges simultaneously with the appropriate state agency and the federal government's Equal

Employment Opportunity Commission (EEOC). The EEOC generally will wait until the state agency has conducted an investigation, then conduct an investigation of its own.

As you might expect, the wheels of government agencies can creak along at their own slow pace. In fact, you might not hear anything for years! Even then, an agency will only determine whether there is reason to believe your charge is true. Therefore, if you are anxious for justice, you should request that the EEOC issue you a notice 180 days after you file your charge.

IF YOU'RE IN THE RIGHT

If the EEOC determines that your complaint is valid, it will first attempt to mediate the dispute between you and the employer. If an agreement can't be reached, the Commission will either file its own suit or issue you a letter giving you the right to sue the employer. You must file your suit within 90 days of receiving such a letter.

If you win your lawsuit, don't expect to receive a colossal jury award. The most you'll probably get from the employer is the equivalent of a year's salary.

ONE LAST WORD

None of the information or advice in this chapter should be taken as legal advice. I am not an attorney. If you feel a prospective employer is guilty of discrimination, your first step should be to contact the appropriate government agencies, as well as an attorney, to accurately assess your rights and options under federal law and the laws and regulations in your state and industry.

TIPS FOR FENDING OFF ILLEGAL QUESTIONS

- **KNOW YOUR RIGHTS.** Do some research to find out what questions are out of bounds in your particular state, industry, or profession.

- **DON'T OPEN THE DOOR** for the interviewer. Let him get it himself! That is, don't bring up subjects you don't want to talk about. If you do, the interviewer is likely to ask what would otherwise have been illegal questions . . . if you hadn't opened the door first.

- **CHANGE THE SUBJECT.** If you feel that the interviewer is asking you questions that shouldn't be asked, the first step is to try to shrug them off and change the direction of the conversation.

- **GIVE THEM THE BENEFIT OF THE DOUBT.** After all, you are here because you want the job. So it's up to you to weigh your personal reactions to certain searching questions against your desire to have this job. Many hiring managers may not realize they are in the wrong. Give them the benefit of the doubt.

- **WARN THE INTERVIEWER** . . . subtly. Tell the interviewer in a non-threatening way that you know the questions he or she is asking are inappropriate. This should deliver the message that you know your rights and aren't willing to be a victim of discrimination.

- **END THE INTERVIEW.** If the interviewer refuses to back off, end the interview quickly. After all, would you really want to work at a company or for a person capable of such narrow-minded attitudes? If you think you have a strong case, look into bringing formal charges against the company and the interviewer.

That's a Wrap!

kay, you've made it this far, you must have the job by now. Anyway, there's absolutely no way to mess it up at this point, right?

Don't be so quick to relax. The closing questions of an interview should be handled with care. In short, there are still likely to be some tough questions ahead. Here goes:

 ARE YOU WILLING TO TRAVEL?

WHAT DO THEY WANT TO HEAR?

Yes, of course you are. Your family understands the demands of your career and is supportive when you need to spend some time away from home. Does that mean you want to be away three weeks out of four? Probably not. Unless you are unwilling to travel at all, don't let this question cost you the job. (If the job requires far more travel than you are prepared for, what are you doing on the interview? And if the heavy travel requirements are a complete shock, why didn't you learn about them beforehand?)

The more travel is an inherent part of the job, the more likely the interviewer will ask this question early in the process, so as to immediately eliminate home-bound candidates.

 ## ARE YOU WILLING TO RELOCATE?

 ## WHAT DO THEY WANT TO HEAR?

If you really are, say so:

> *"Absolutely. In fact, I would look forward to the chance to live elsewhere and experience a different lifestyle and meet new people."*

If you're not, say so:

> *"Well, not unless the job is so terrific that it would be worth uprooting my family and leaving my relatives and friends. Does this position require a move? I'm obviously very interested in it, so I might consider relocating."*

VARIATION

● *Do you have any location preferences?*

 ## MAY I CONTACT YOUR CURRENT EMPLOYER?

Why do people ask this question? You probably will feel like saying, "Sure, after you give me this job and I don't have to worry about getting canned because I've been out looking for another job."

But you'll sound better saying:

> *"Sure you can—after we come to an agreement. I think it's best if they hear about this from me first."*

MAY I CONTACT YOUR REFERENCES?

 WHAT DO THEY WANT TO HEAR?

"Of course you can." Tell the interviewer that you will get back to him or her with a list of references that afternoon or, if it is already afternoon, the very next day.

Does this stalling make you seem unprepared? Shouldn't you go into the interview with the list ready to hand over to the interviewer?

Frankly, in the world of interviews, stalling for a little time before giving references is SOP (standard operating procedure). The reason you want to wait is so you can tell your prospective references that a call might be coming from Mr. Krueger of Triskaidekaphobia, Inc. If your references are indeed going to say wonderful things about you, they should be prepared to do so.

Caveat: Employers are growing more reluctant to provide references because of a rise in the number of claims of defamation and misrepresentation. Because job references are partially privileged communications, it's a good idea to try to get an inside line on what is being said about you to a prospective employer. As an applicant, you may be able to approach a current or former employer to work out a narrative job reference that is accurate and amenable to both of you. With your consent and involvement, former employers may be more willing to discuss your strengths and weaknesses, as well as the circumstances surrounding your departure, in a positive light.

 IS THERE ANYTHING ELSE ABOUT YOU I SHOULD KNOW?

 WHAT DO THEY WANT TO HEAR?

You might not think you have anything else left to say, but you should. This is your chance—beautifully presented on a silver platter—to close the sale. You'd be a fool to turn it down.

Develop a short answer to this question, one that plays upon your strengths, accomplishments, skills, and areas of knowledge. For example,

> *"Mr. Krueger, I think we've covered everything. But I want to reemphasize the key strengths that I would bring to this position:*
>
> *Experience. The job I'm currently in is quite similar to this one, and I would be excited by the chance to apply what I've learned at WidgetLand to working for your company.*
>
> *Management skills. I run a department almost equal in size to this one. I'm a fair and effective supervisor.*
>
> *A record of success. I've won two prestigious industry awards. I would bring that creativity here.*
>
> *Enthusiasm. I am very excited about the prospect of working with you here at Triskaidekaphobia. When do you expect to make a decision?"*

This type of answer should underline the points that you have been trying to make throughout the entire interview. By ending with a question, you ask Mr. Krueger to take some action. This is an effective selling technique that should give you a good indication of your chances of getting the job.

VARIATIONS

● *Why should I hire you?*

● *If you were me, would you hire you?*

MONEY TALKS

No one likes to talk about money during an interview. It seems indelicate, somehow. But that doesn't mean you should avoid it completely. Just remember that timing is everything.

My own rule of thumb is simple: Don't discuss dollars and cents until after you've convinced the interviewer that you're the best person for the job.

That's why I've relegated the first question on salary to near the end of the final chapter. Until you've made it over all the other interview hurdles, the interviewer is still assessing your ability. And he or she is probably still seeing other contenders as well, some whose talent may come cheaper than your own.

But even if an interviewer tries to pressure you into revealing a specific number early in the game, avoid committing yourself. Instead, name a very broad range. You might say, "I believe a fair wage for this kind of position would be between \$30,000 and \$40,000."

Be sure the bottom end of that range is no less than the minimum salary you would be willing to accept for the position.

Once the employer has made his decision, you'll be in a much stronger bargaining position.

 WHAT SORT OF SALARY ARE YOU LOOKING FOR?

 WHAT DO THEY WANT TO HEAR?

You should have a pretty good idea of what your particular market will bear. If you don't know the particular salary ranges in your area (city and state) and industry, do some research. Make sure you know whether these figures represent just dollars or a compensation package, which may include insurance, retirement programs, and other value-added benefits.

If you're a woman, make sure you know what men are making doing the same job. You're bound to find a discrepancy. But you should request and expect to earn an equivalent salary, regardless of what female predecessors may have earned.

Even if you've been out of a job for months, this is not the time or place to let your desperation show, so avoid gushing, "Gee, this job sounds so gosh-darned wonderful I can't believe you're going to pay me anything! Just give me an office and a phone, and I'll work for the sheer fun of it!"

Have confidence in your own worth. By this time, you've worked hard to sell the interviewer on your value as a future employee. Just remind him of what he's already decided.

VARIATION

● *What do you think this job should pay?*

 THE SALARY YOU'RE ASKING FOR IS NEAR THE TOP OF THE RANGE FOR THIS JOB. WHY SHOULD WE PAY YOU THIS MUCH?

 WHAT DO THEY WANT TO HEAR?

Remind the employer of the cost savings and other benefits she'll enjoy when you come on board. For example, you might say:

> *"I was able to cut my previous employer's expenses by 10 percent by negotiating better deals with vendors. I think it's reasonable to expect that any additional salary we agree to would be offset by savings I could bring the company."*

 WHEN CAN YOU START?

 WHAT DO THEY WANT TO HEAR?

If you've been laid off or fired, you can start immediately, of course.

But if you're still working for someone else, you should give at least two weeks' notice to your employer, more if you are leaving a position in which you've had considerable responsibility.

As eager as you may be to get started on this new job, I know I don't have to remind you that it's never wise to burn bridges. You never know when you might have to cross one of them again! So be as accommodating as you can. For example, offer to help find and train your replacement.

If it will be several weeks before you can assume your new responsibilities full-time, offer to begin studying literature or files in your off-hours. Or come into the office in the evening or on a weekend to meet members of the staff and begin to familiarize yourself with the lay of the land. You might even be called on to attend a company event or seminar.

 RED LIGHT

Although it may reflect your true feelings about the job, saying you "aren't sure" when you can start implies to me you "aren't sure" about taking the job.

Don't ever admit you can't start for several weeks because you want to take a vacation. I can empathize with someone who feels the need to "recover" from a bitter job experience before punching the clock at a new one, but there's just something that sticks in my craw about such an answer. Perhaps it's the feeling that you're already putting your own needs above mine; maybe it's a real hardship for me to wait four weeks. Maybe it's my own idiosyncrasy, but I really hate to hear about someone planning a vacation before starting to work for me.

 IS THERE ANYTHING THAT WILL INHIBIT YOU FROM TAKING THIS JOB IF OFFERED?

 WHAT DO THEY WANT TO HEAR?

"Absolutely not."

The interviewer is attempting to do everything in his power to ascertain whether you'll accept the job if offered and actually show up on the start date. But there is no way he can guarantee either. All he can hope to do is give you another opportunity to voice a previously hidden concern—too small a salary, a poor benefits package, a lousy cubicle, reporting to too many people, inadequate support, unrealistic sales or profit expectations, and the like.

 ## ARE YOU CONSIDERING ANY OTHER OFFERS RIGHT NOW?

 ## WHAT DO THEY WANT TO HEAR?

This is another closing question I like to ask early in the process so I know what I'm up against. Of course, this is presuming that an honest answer is good for you, which, frankly, it probably isn't. Unless you believe the interviewer will respond positively to such an admission, you should play your cards very close to the vest. You'll probably gain nothing by admitting you have other irons in the fire, so why stir up the coals?

VARIATIONS

- *Tell me about the other offers you're considering.*

- *How does this job compare to others for which you are interviewing?*

APRÈS-INTERVIEW ETIQUETTE

Once you step out from under the bright lights and shake hands with the interviewer, it will probably take all the composure you can muster not to kick up your heels and run out of the office.

But in your haste, don't forget that the process is not quite over. Whether you're waiting by the phone for an offer or off to your next "ordeal," there are a few standard rules of etiquette you should follow:

- Ask when the hiring decision will be made. If you don't get word by the indicated date, it's perfectly acceptable to call the employer to inquire about the status of the position.

- Write a thank-you note. Make it short and sweet. Thank the interviewer for taking the time to meet with you. Then restate your interest in the company and the position, and find a way to remind the interviewer of how you can use your skill and experience to address one of the key requirements of the job. Type it in a business-style format, and be sure there are no typographical or spelling errors.

- Remember that if you met with more than one interviewer, you should send thank-you letters to each person with whom you talked.

- Many counselors now condone an E-mail thank-you note. The benefit, of course, is that you can have one in the interviewer's computer minutes after you walk out the door. But get a feel for the interviewer; if she is seldom online, she may consider an E-mail impersonal. Even if you e-mail the interviewer, I would also send a paper copy of your letter.

FINISHING TOUCHES

● **NOURISH YOUR NETWORK.** If a colleague or former associate referred you to the company or arranged a personal introduction with the interviewer or hiring manager, be sure to drop that person a note of thanks as well.

● **REPLAY THE HIGHS AND THE LOWS.** What went well during the interviewing process? What could you have done better? The point is not to berate yourself for what you did or didn't say. You merely want to make sure you keep doing the things that worked—and working on what didn't—so you can ace your next interview.

● **REWRITE YOUR RESUME.** Did the interviewer have any questions that you could clarify through your resume? Did you find yourself talking about accomplishments you forgot to include? If so, now is the time to revise your resume, before you send it out again.

● **KEEP IN TOUCH.** The hiring process can move at a snail's pace in corporate America. Often, the larger the corporation, the slower the pace. So don't panic if a week or two passes before you hear anything. No news may be good news. If time stretches on, it's okay to call to find out if the job has been filled. Use the opportunity to remind the employer of your interest and qualifications. (But I wouldn't call back more than three times if you don't get a response. Not getting a response should lead you to get the message.)

- **ACCEPT . . . IN YOUR OWN TIME AND ON YOUR OWN TERMS.** Never accept an offer at the time it is tendered. Take a day or two to think about it. Tell the interviewer when you will announce your decision. If you do decide to refuse the offer, politely tell the employer why you don't feel you can accept the position.

- **CONGRATULATE YOURSELF.** You made it through one of life's more stressful experiences with flying colors. You've proven you're a real pro. Now you're on your way.

APPENDIX

---

20 Smart Questions to Ask on Your Interview

Crafting concise, targeted, enthusiastic, and positive responses to the interviewer's questions gives you an opportunity to demonstrate your knowledge of the company and industry and to show how your qualifications would help you fit right in. *Asking* concise, targeted, and well-crafted questions gives you additional chances to demonstrate the extent of your research, to build on whatever rapport you've established, and to align what you know and can do with what the company needs.

These questions, by their very nature, proclaim that *you are interested*. Likewise, the complete *lack* of questions will undoubtedly convince most interviewers that you are *not* interested. Asking questions early and often transforms a stilted, traditional "Q & A" session—with you being the "A"—into a *conversation*. And a conversation is how you explore areas of common interest, trade comments, and chat rather than "talk." In other words, the way you establish the chemistry that is one of the vital factors in landing any job!

The first six questions may seem odd; they are certainly not questions you would ask any interviewer. But, in my mind, they are far more important than the other 14 questions—*they are the questions you must ask yourself before accepting any job.*

1. *Can* I do the job?

Are you really qualified? Be honest with yourself, because if the answer is "no," sooner or later it will not be a secret to your boss!

2. Do I *want* the job?

They may love and want you, but you'd better be sure this is a job you can be passionate about. If not, but you plan to take it anyway, you should at least be honest and *know* you are compromising for a reason that is valid to you . . . like, you have to eat.

3. Does this job fit in with my long-range plans?

The more solid and thought-out your long-range goals, the easier it is to create a directed and targeted career *path* rather than simply a series of jobs that fail to build upon one another. Just as you can and should take charge of the interview, you must control your own career path. Make sure you have honestly analyzed whether this job fits in with your own goals.

4. Will I fit in?

Did you like your prospective boss? Did you like the people you'll be working with? Those you'll be managing? A job is not simply a set of functions; it's a collection of environments created by all the other people that work at the company. You may be totally qualified for and challenged by the job itself, but if you can't stand any of the people, how long do you think you're going to last?

5. Can I live on what they want to pay me?

If your ideal job won't even pay the rent or the mortgage, you have a problem. But the biggest problem is if you haven't bothered to think about your financial needs at all.

6. Do I feel secure taking a job at _____?

Doubling your salary may be wonderful. Stock options could make you rich. Or you could find yourself back on the street in a month if you haven't bothered to ask yourself this question. Always evaluate the compensation package in concert with your analysis of the health of the company. It doesn't matter how much they promise to pay you if they're heading toward bankruptcy.

Presuming you have positively answered the first six questions and are prepared to take the job if it is offered, use the next 14 questions to cement your position and assure yourself that you are making the right decision.

7. Given my qualifications, skills, and experience, do you have any concerns about my ability to become an important member of this company?

Probably not—if you didn't meet the summary of qualifications forwarded to Human Resources, you wouldn't be talking to anyone. But it never hurts to ask a question designed to uncover hidden objections.

8. What are your goals in the next few years?

This question can be directed to the Human Resources screener or the hiring manager. If you did research on this topic prior to the interview, you should have information to pose an informed follow-up question once you receive an answer.

9. Do you anticipate any cutbacks in the near future and, if you do, how will they impact my department or position?

While hiring new employees is typically a sign of a company's prosperity, the past few years have given us examples of businesses that have added too many staff too quickly . . . and had to "divest" themselves of many of those new hires soon thereafter. Although the person answering this question cannot predict the future, his or her answer, combined with your own analysis of industry trends, should give you a decent indication of whether there are layoffs in the company's future.

10. Could you describe a typical day in this position?

This ought to clear up any misconceptions you have about the job. It can be used to address questions about travel, telecommuting, and interactivity. If you are someone who enjoys an interactive working environment, you will want to know whether the prospective job keeps you chained to your cube all day, with all communication occurring by E-mail, or involves a steady stream of face-to-face meetings, client contact, and a constantly ringing telephone.

11. Why is this job available? Is this a new position?

New positions imply growth. Any company growing now may well be one you want to work for. A new position may also give you more input into your job description and duties. On the other hand, you could also find out that the job is available because the last three people who held the position quit or got fired, which should give you pause.

12. How would my performance be measured in this position? How is the department's performance measured?

Particularly if the salary is not exactly what you desire, the performance review process will indicate how the company handles bonuses and raises. The answer to this question will tell you what is expected of you, as well as how much responsibility you have over the rest of the department and how departmental performance is tied to your individual performance.

13. How would you describe your management style?

Even if you are comfortable with the job, the department, and the company—and have had most or all of your questions about them answered—never underestimate the importance of your boss's "style," the corporate culture, and how you will mesh with both.

14. What kinds of people seem to succeed in this company?

This is a not-so-veiled attempt to define yourself according to the attributes the manager cites, presuming, of course, that the type of person she describes isn't so remote from your own personality as to be laughable.

15. Could you explain the organizational structure of the department and its primary functions and responsibilities?

Once you have established in your own mind that you are truly interested in the company, you will want to ask detailed questions designed to elicit specific information about the department, the job, and the people. Answers to these questions will add to what you already know about the job and clarify how the company is set up, whom you report to, who reports to you, and how you will (hopefully) fit in.

16. What are the things you would most like to see changed in this department?

Once this question is answered, you should follow up by describing how you are qualified to implement such changes and how you will flourish in the new environment. The answer should also give an indication whether the changes (and the management implementing them!) are reasonable and what types of problems already exist at your potential new job.

17. Is there anything else I can tell you that would help you make the decision to hire me?

This directly implies your interest in the position, puts you in the position of helping rather than selling, and attempts to close the sale all at the same time. There is, of course, a not-so-fine line between appearing confident and being an arrogant boor. Adjust the level of aggressiveness to the tone of the interview. If you've done a good job establishing rapport with the interviewer and are having a comfortable, conversational interview, there's no reason to come off like a fire-breathing dragon when it's time to close the sale.

18. When do you expect to make a final decision and fill the position?

Frankly, even an aggressive sales type should avoid being *too* pushy. Pressuring an interviewer for a decision by a specific day (or, worse, immediately) may be going overboard at all but the most Type-A companies. However, you can use this question to convey your strong interest in the job. It may also make you seem a more attractive candidate, especially if you mention that you are only trying to pin down a date so you can get back to all of your other job offers.

19. Are there any upcoming events occurring before my start date in which I could participate?

The more social, the better. You really want to see your boss, peers, and subordinates once they've "let their hair down." (If they remain stiff and formal even at social events, there's a message there too!) So a company picnic is great. A departmental "let's-have-a-beer-together" Friday night is nice, though socially tough if you're not a butterfly. It would be most beneficial if you could attend one of these before you make a decision, but that's unlikely. However, if there's a big press conference or similar corporate event, you could always ask to attend. A little exposure to the "big wigs" to see what they're really saying in public, as opposed to what they told you in the interview, may prove enlightening.

20. What could I do to jump-start my entry into the department?

This question will confirm to the interviewer that he has made the right decision. Look at that passion! That interest! That aggression!

INDEX

Extracurricular activities, 73–74
Eye contact, 7, 48

F

Failure
  meaning of, 69–70
  personal experience of, 92–93,
    119
  See also Weaknesses
Fair Employment Practices Com-
  mission, 179
Family, 167–169, 180–183
"Favorite job" question, 87–88
Federal Americans with Disabilities
  Act, 187
Federal Deposit Insurance Act, 190
Federal Immigration Reform and
  Control Act (1986), 184
Financial experience, 121–122
Financial situation, personal, 189
Fired, experience of being, 128,
  133–134
Firing employees, experience with,
  122–123
Fit, with company/department,
  37–38, 63, 98–99, 144, 159,
  206, 208–209
"Five years from now" question,
  61–62
  green lights for, 62–63
  red lights for, 63–64
  variations on, 64–65

G

Generalizations, avoidance of, 40,
  46, 58, 63, 109
Giving notice, 200
Goals, 61–65, 145–146, 160–161, 206
Graduate school data input sheet, 26
Green lights
  activities, 169
  company conducting interview,
    151, 158

current job, 130–133, 135, 139
details, 116–117
education, 76–77, 80–82
goals, 62–63
"Tell me about yourself" question, 52–56
work experience, 86, 88–90, 93,
  95–96, 105–107, 110, 119,
  122–123
Grooming, 4
Growth, personal, 71

H

Health, 167, 187–188
High school data input sheet, 23
Hiring employees, experience with,
  123–124
HIV, 187–188
Hobbies. *See* Activities; Interests
Honesty, 6, 48
Human resources professionals, as
  interviewers, 34–35
Human screen, interviewer as,
  34–35
Humility, 71, 77
Humor, inappropriateness of, 75
Hypothetical questions, 45–47, 104,
  147–148

I

Ice-breakers, 50, 151, 176–177
Ideal job questions, 160–163
Illegal aliens, 184
Illegal questions, 84, 167, 178–193
  legal action based on, 191–192
  responses to, 181–182, 190–191,
    193
Inconsistency, in answers/resume,
  86–87, 103, 116, 135, 136,
  142–143
Innovation. *See* Creativity
Interests, personal, 16–17, 169–170
Internships, 80–81

R

Reading habits, 177
Red lights
  activities, 74–75
  appearance, 4
  behavior, 6, 7
  clarifying questions, 58–59, 86
  clothing, 5
  company conducting
    interview, 158
  current job, 130–132, 134–135,
    139–140
  defensiveness, 8
  details, 117
  education, 77–78, 80, 81, 83
  enthusiasm, lack of, 58
  eye contact, 7, 56
  generalization, 58, 63
  goals, 63–64
  human screens, 34
  identical answers, 41
  lack of preparation, 8
  language, 56
  late for interview, 4
  loyalty lacking, 132
  lunch, 9
  lying, 6, 132
  manager-conducted interviews, 36
  negativity, 7, 77, 87, 90,
    130–131, 134
  nervousness, 58
  overconfidence, 8, 64
  personal revelations, 6
  relevance, lack of, 58
  smoking, 5
  starting date, 200
  success, 68
  telephone interviews, 32–33
  unsuitable answers, 9–10
  weaknesses, 65–66
  work experience, 86–88, 90–97,
    105, 119–120

References, employment, 195–196
Refusing an offer, 204
Relationship skills, 96–97,
    105–107, 144
Relevance of answers, 58
Religion, 186–187
Relocation, 181, 195
Research on companies, 71, 97–98,
    151–152, 158
Responsibilities, job, 14, 134–135
Responsibility, taking, 69–70, 83, 93
Resumes
  answers consistent with,
    86–87, 135
  customized, 73
  focusing on positive aspects of, 55
  of inexperienced applicants, 72
  revising, based on interviews, 203
Risk, attitude toward, 104, 113

S

Salary, 77, 198–199, 206
Sales, 126–127
Salesperson, interviewee as, 12–13,
    19–20, 38, 209–210
Self-presentation
  "best friend" question and, 61
  education question and, 75
  exaggerated, 38, 91–92
  preparation for, 12–20, 57,
    196–197
  "Tell me about yourself"
    question and, 50–52, 59–60
  tips on, 171
Self-promotion, excessive, 38, 91–92
Self-reflection, 206–207
Sexual orientation, 185
Skills, job, 15, 118–119
Smiling, 48
Smoking, 5
Specifics. *See* Details
Starting date, 199–200

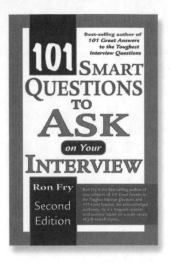

Best-selling author Ron Fry's 101 Series shows savvy job seekers how to turn even the most challenging job interviews into opportunities. Each book has been updated and revised to include more in-depth coverage of the interview process, various kinds of interviews job seekers may encounter, and tips for preparing and sending electronic job applications.

101 Smart Questions to Ask on Your Interview, 2E
224 pp., 5 1/2" x 8 1/2", softcover, 2007
ISBN: 1-4180-4001-0 • List Price: $11.99 Z

101 Smart Questions to Ask on Your Interview delivers practical advice on wrapping up the interview and making yourself stand out.

KEY FEATURES
- Top tips from best selling career author, to get in the door and make the most of every interview
- Eye-catching series layout and design directs readers to key information and invites browsing
- Forms and checklists for preparing and organizing skills and experience